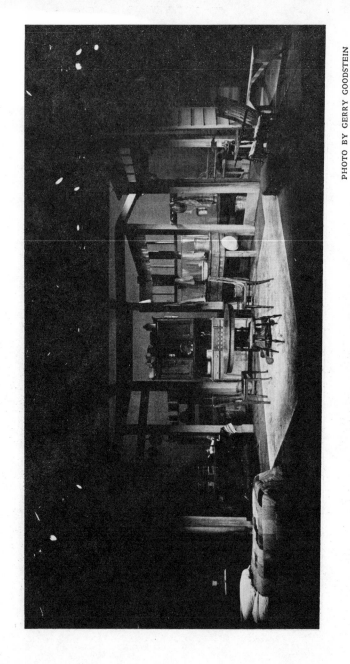

Setting for the Manhattan Theatre Club production of "Artichoke." Designed by Fred Voelpel.

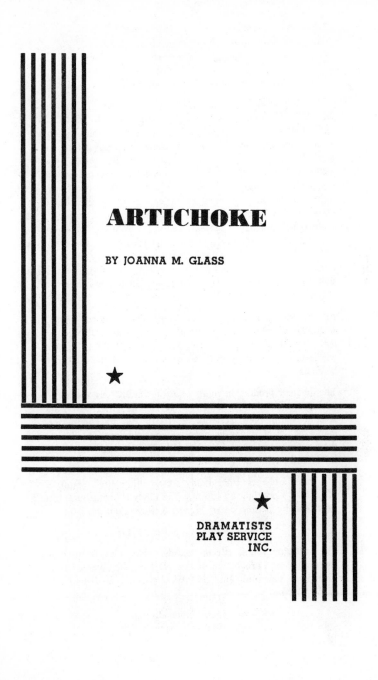

ARTICHOKE

BY JOANNA M. GLASS

DRAMATISTS
PLAY SERVICE
INC.

SOUND EFFECTS RECORDS

The following sound effects records, which may be used in connection with production of this play, can be obtained from Thomas J. Valentino, Inc., 151 West 46th Street, New York, N. Y. 10036.

No. 4100—Door closing
No. 5041—Car stopping

ARTICHOKE was first presented at the Long Wharf Theatre, in New Haven, Connecticut, by special arrangement with Elliot Martin, on October 17, 1975. It was directed by Arvin Brown; the setting was by David Jenkins; costumes were by Bill Walker; the lighting was by Ronald Wallace; and the stage manager was Anne Keefe. The cast, in order of speaking, was as follows:

JAKE, a neighbor .... Louis Beachner
ARCHIE, a neighbor .... James Greene
MARGARET .... Colleen Dewhurst
GRAMPA, her father .... Emery Battis
WALTER, her husband .... Rex Robbins
LILY AGNES, his daughter .... Ellin Ruskin
GIBSON McFARLAND, Margaret's distant cousin ...... Brian Murray

ARTICHOKE was presented in New York City, at the Manhattan Theatre Club, on February 13, 1979. It was directed by Lynne Meadow; the setting was by Fred Voelpel; costumes were by Patricia McGourty; the lighting was by Jennifer Tipton; and the production stage manager was Jason La Padura. The cast, in order of appearance, was as follows:

JAKE .... Daniel Keyes
ARCHIE .... James Greene
MARGARET MORLEY .... Patricia Elliott
WALTER MORLEY .... Rex Robbins
LILY AGNES .... Amanda Michael Plummer
GRAMPS .... Michael Higgins
GIBSON McFARLAND .... Nicholas Hormann

3

Place: The Saskatchewan Prairie

Time: Summer

ACT I
Mid-July

ACT II
Three days later

CAST

JAKE and ARCHIE: Two sixty year old farmers. They are neighbors of the Morley family.

WALTER MORLEY: A large, appealing farmer, about forty.

MARGARET: Walter's wife. Mid-thirties.

LILY AGNES: Walter's "natural" child, fourteen.

GRAMPS: Margaret's father, late sixties.

GIBSON McFARLAND: An attractive visiting professor, about forty.

ARTICHOKE

ACT ONE

The play is set on a wheat farm on the Saskatchewan prairie. The farm is large—five hundred acres. The main set is the Morley kitchen, a large, homey, pleasant room that is clearly the center of activity.

There are two entrances to the kitchen. One is Down Left, leading to the stairs and the parlor, the other is Center, leading to the back porch.

There is a large old table used for canning, baking and meals. There should be, along one wall, a "Toronto couch." This is a long day-bed, covered with a spread during the day. These beds, or cots, are not generally very useful in summer, but are an ideal place for the sick, in winter. There is a small chest of drawers near the couch. This would be used, eventually, for Gibson's belongings.

The action of the play moves from the Morley kitchen to Jake and Archie's farm. This second set is simply a platform with a table and three chairs on it, and stacks of newspapers. It may either be a separate entity, or it may be incorporated into the central set through the use of a scrim. The lights come up on Jake and Archie's table. They are drinking tea, and reading newspapers.

These two are practically identical in appearance and are actually indistinguishable throughout the play. Both wear boots, dark socks, denim overalls. They are bachelors who combined their acreage and have lived together for

5

thirty years. Their humor is straight-forward, droll, understated.

JAKE. Oh, Archie, I must say you make a good *cuppa!*

ARCHIE. Thank you, Jake. Thank you. (*Archie lights a pipe, turns to the audience, and puts his paper down.*) We always like to read the newspapers.

JAKE. We read a great deal. We toil from sun to sun, and then we read. We try to read mostly about people whose lives are more colorful than our own.

ARCHIE. You can always depend on headlines. Damn fool people making damn fool headlines.

JAKE. Damn fool headlines, very often caused by scandal.

ARCHIE. *Sexual* scandal, more often than not.

JAKE. For instance, in England. They seem to run amok at the highest levels. They were that stiff upper lip, and then, somewhere's around middle age, the pressure builds up and they can't stand it. And they run amok in the most peculiar ways.

ARCHIE. Just recently, there was this fellow, Jeremy Thorpe. He made awful good reading.

JAKE. Oh, that man's exploits would make an apple blush.

ARCHIE. We've noticed a pattern with the men in these articles. They're born and bred to be first class in the head, but they're always at a loss where the body's concerned.

JAKE. And the mystery is, they never seem to learn that dirty linen always stinks. There was another one, some years ago—uh—

ARCHIE. Profumo.

JAKE. That's it. He got tangled up with a girl named Christine. *Christine.* Whose mother must have had something Christian in mind, when she named her.

ARCHIE. Her friend made the headlines, too. Her friend was Randy, I think—

JAKE. Oh, certainly her friend was randy, but I think her *name* was *Mandy.*

ARCHIE. Yes, that's right. Her name was Mandy. (*Pause.*) Well, it's been some years. What was touching, though, was the way Mrs. Profumo took it. He was married to that pretty Valerie Hobson, if you remember. And she stood beside him for photographs, after his fall. She linked her arm in his and held her head

6

up high and stood straight and tall. And it was touching. Because what they presented was a *united front*.

JAKE. A united front when the heat was on—

ARCHIE. She kept her head when all about was losing theirs. (*Pause.*) But the most *disturbing* headline, was when it all came out about F.D.R. and the social secretary.

JAKE. *Her* name was Lucy. Such an innocent name—Lucy.

ARCHIE. They say she was with him when he died, down there in Warm Springs, Georgia.

JAKE. It broke our hearts to hear it, because we all had such a high regard for Eleanor.

ARCHIE. There was a woman!

JAKE. Aye! Do you remember the photo of her down there in the coal mines with the gas lamp on her brow? And somebody said, "What is it, Eleanor, that makes you the great lady that you are?" And she said, "I have always been curious."

ARCHIE. So it broke our hearts to hear it that F.D.R. had taken the fall with the social secretary.

JAKE. Of course, there were some who were encouraged at the news.

ARCHIE. Oh, yes, there's always some. The handicapped across the land were much encouraged at the news.

JAKE. And Eleanor never made a peep. She stood straight and tall, just like she didn't know, and she continued to pose for photographs.

ARCHIE. (*Transition.*) Down the road apiece we've got some neighbors named Morley. (*Spotlight up on Margaret, in the kitchen.*) The wife is Margaret Morley. Mar-gar-et. She says the name is from the Greek. It means, "a pearl."

JAKE. And that is what she is! Oh, many a mustard plaster's been laid on our chests—in the dead of winter—by Margaret Morley—

ARCHIE. (*Euphorically.*) The pearl!! (*Spotlight up on Walter.*) Now, the husband is Walter Morley. A fine looking man, even now. An ordinary man, a farmer, nothing in common with politicians. But still, a man. And he took the fall. And there was scandal.

JAKE. Fifteen years ago he married Margaret. She was a town

7

girl, better educated than Walter. She was something of a catch, too, because her Dad was Mayor of our little town of Raglan. (*Spotlight off Margaret and Walter.*)

ARCHIE. Walter had a terrible reputation for hell-raising, so it was hoped that marriage would settle him down. And, indeed, it did, for the first year. Then, in the second year, the Morley's well ran dry.

JAKE. It was then Walter engaged the services of a traveling water witch.

ARCHIE. A water witch is a female who believes she's *inspired* when it comes to predicting the whereabouts of water. They're all crazy as loons and they carry a stick—

JAKE. Sometimes called a "wand"—

ARCHIE. —about so long, with a curve in it. This curve automatically turns downward if there's water below ground.

JAKE. Well, Walter and the witch roamed his land for a week. Her wand eventually did turn down, and then she went away, and Walter started digging. But that, of course, wasn't the end of it. (*Spot up on Lily Agnes, reading.*)

ARCHIE. What happened next was Lily Agnes.

JAKE. Nine months after Walter got his well, somebody delivered a baby onto Margaret Morley's doorstep. The note only had an "X" on it. We all examined the note, and we all agreed it was the mark of the water witch.

ARCHIE. Margaret took the babe in, and she christened her Lily Agnes. And we've all, since then, had a very high regard for Margaret Morley.

WALTER. (*To Lily Agnes.*) I'm going out to milk. You come along and fetch the eggs. (*No response.*) Lily Agnes, put down that goddamn book, and fetch the eggs. (*Walter and Lily Agnes exit.*)

JAKE. Lily Agnes is very dear, but she's not quite right. She's never been sent to school 'cause at school they'd poke fun. Margaret tutored her at home with great success. Around here we say that Lily Agnes is fourteen, going on forty-five.

ARCHIE. Now. There was no united front. Margaret didn't link her arm in Walter's, and she never stood for photographs. She gave all the love she had to give to Lily Agnes. And she banished Walter out to the smokehouse. He's made a nice little nest out there, but sometimes he says he feels more like a monk, in a cell. That's when he goes to see a woman in Raglan.

JAKE. Seldom more than once a month—

ARCHIE. Just for . . . relief. (*Spotlight up on Gramps.*)

JAKE. Margaret's old Dad lives there, too. Gramps Ferguson. He was Mayor of Raglan for a total of eight years. Gramps was widowed early, and he not only raised Margaret all by himself, but he done a wonderful thing—

ARCHIE. He took in an orphan boy named Gibson, when Gibson's folks was killed in a train wreck. We never met Gibson, but it looks like we're going to.

JAKE. It's July now. The wheat's in. The grasshoppers is jumping and spitting. Down the road at the Morley place they're all excited because he's coming—the orphan boy—

ARCHIE. All the way from Vancouver—

JAKE. In a great big air-O-plane. We didn't know why he's coming back—

ARCHIE. But it's very likely we'll find out. (*The lights dim on Jake and Archie and rise on the Morley kitchen. Margaret is standing at a mirror. She is squinting, pulling out grey hairs. Gramps sits nearby, wearing a suit and tie.*)

MARGARET. Ouch! Stubborn little buggers.

GRAMPS. What are?

MARGARET. Grey hairs.

GRAMPS. They say when you pull one, seven come to its funeral.

MARGARET. It's better than the dye bottle. Nellie Link says that dye concoction is pure ammonia. Peels your scalp right off in chunks.

GRAMPS. Margaret, if you don't stop yanking out hairs, Gibson will think you've been scalped by an Indian.

MARGARET. (*Very displeased with her appearance.*) Have you looked at me lately? (*She waits.*) Obviously not. My breasts are sagging, my belly's got no elastic left, my peaches and cream have turned to horsehide. (*Pause.*) How can I have all these laugh lines when I haven't laughed in years?

GRAMPS. You ought to buy one of those moisturizing night creams.

MARGARET. I won't do it! Four dollars the ounce, and Nellie Link says all they are is pig fat. Perfumed pig fat. I won't do it.

9

GRAMPS. Margaret, sometimes I think you're just downright cheap.

MARGARET. And how do I come by THAT, I wonder?

GRAMPS. I was never cheap. I was perhaps . . . frugal.

MARGARET. You were cheap. It's your Scots blood. (*Pause.*) Do you know why Scotsmen have big noses?

GRAMPS. Uh-uh.

MARGARET. Because AIR IS FREE! (*They both laugh, then Margaret goes off to a lament.*) Oh, there's a clarity today that I just can't stand! A clarity about my life. It must have to do with Gibson's coming. (*She turns, dramatically, toward the porch.*) It's the porch for me, and a wicker rocker. A thin grey bun at the back of my head, and great bulging bunions stretching out my shoes. I'll sit there shelling peas, day after day, with by gnarled, arthritic hands.

GRAMPS. What I love about you, Margaret, is your gift for understatement. (*Transition.*) Poor, poor Gibson. He should have been forewarned. I wonder what he's going to make of all this.

MARGARET. A lot more sense than we do! He has a Ph.D., you know. He's become an international authority on Alexander Pope. Gibson is no stranger to the ways of the world!

GRAMPS. The city world, Margaret! Vancouver! And if he can't deal with *that*, what's he going to make of these shenanigans? My God! Lily Agnes, toting around that old copy of Emily Post. You. Fidgeting. Waxing the finish off all the furniture. Walter, out in the smokehouse.

MARGARET. (*Waving a letter.*) Gibson says he's coming to visit because he has a bad case of *weltschmerz*. Do you know what that is?

GRAMPS. Uh-uh.

MARGARET. *World pain.* That means Gibson has suffered. And you know as well as anyone, there's been some suffering here. So he'll understand. He won't be shocked. (*Pause.*) If you have to trust your secrets with someone, can you think of anyone better than a person afflicted with *weltschmerz*? (*Distantly, we hear Walter, coming from the barn, singing:*)

WALTER.

> The old grey mare went phfft on the whiffle tree
> Phfft on the whiffle tree

10

Phffft on the whiffle tree—

MARGARET. And here he comes. Caruso.

GRAMPS. I wish he wouldn't sing that vulgar song.

MARGARET. His mind's been stuck for years in the great, dank hole of bodily functions. He thinks of nothing else.

GRAMPS. Neither do you.

MARGARET. Oh, I do! Yes, I do! I think of many other things. I think of shiny floors and clean white muslin on the windows. I think of meals, hundreds of meals every year. Peeling and paring and chopping. Parboil, simmer, saute. THOUSANDS of meals, every year. I think of stitching and mending and baking and canning. In the fall I think of preparing the root cellar. I think of petunias, all sticky and gay in spring. I think of Lily Agnes, and what to teach her. And when I do think of bodily functions, I think of a man and a woman. And there's a silver moon, and she has just recently bathed in lavender. She has lovely white shoulders and soft, curving breasts. And he wears something rough—not denim or chambray. An English tweed. A small, natty houndstooth. And he has a terrible, terrible need for sanctuary. (*Pause.*) When WALTER thinks of bodily functions, he sings. About a farting old horse and a whiffle tree. (*Walter enters with a bang. He wears his barn clothes.*)

WALTER. Well sir, it's arrived, ain't it? The red letter day. The Doctor of Philosophy is coming.

MARGARET. Any time now. You finished early today.

WALTER. Lick and a promise today, that's all. (*Pause.*) You've fixed up today, haven't you, Margaret?

MARGARET. Yes.

WALTER. Got a girdle on.

MARGARET. Yes.

WALTER. You're mighty attractive! If I didn't know better, I'd never think you were the mother of a fourteen year old child.

MARGARET. The point is, you didn't know better. So I'm the mother of a fourteen year old child.

WALTER. Ah, yes! (*As if reciting.*) Walter sinned ages ago, and Margaret rose to the occasion. What are you going to tell Gibson? (*Margaret scowls and doesn't answer.*)

GRAMPS. I guess we'll tell him Walter sinned, ages ago, and Margaret rose to the occasion.

WALTER. (*Preparing to shave.*) I swear to God, it must be the longest stalemate in the history of man and woman. (*Pause.*) There's something I'd like to know. (*He waits for a reaction. There is none.*) I'd like to know where he's going to sleep. How come you haven't talked about that?

MARGARET. We have.

WALTER. Yes, I expect you have. Tell me, if you will, just where the man will lay down his heavy, heavy brain of an evening?

MARGARET. Lily Agnes will move in with Dad, and Gibson will take Lily's room.

WALTER. We want him to have a private room.

MARGARET. Yes, we do.

WALTER. Nothin' but the best for Gibson.

MARGARET. That's right.

WALTER. What about the Toronto couch, down here?

GRAMPS. Walter, we want Gibson to have a private room.

WALTER. Now, listen to me, you two. I ain't having Lily Agnes pushed from pillar to post on account of some screwed up professor. This here Toronto couch is good enough and he should be thankful for that. I mean, he wasn't even *invited*. No word in years and suddenly he's coming for the whole damned summer. They get pushy like that, you know, in the big cities. And it is, after all, MY house. (*Margaret groans.*) And Lily Agnes is, in a manner of speaking, MY daughter. *Technically*, she's more mine than yours. I don't suppose you've asked HER opinion on where she's gonna sleep for the whole damned summer?

MARGARET. Actually, no. If you feel so strongly about it, we'll ask Lily and leave it up to her.

WALTER. I do! I feel strongly about it. I feel goddamn-pissed-off mad about it. (*He returns to shave.*) Jesus, WOMEN! Always telling you where you have to sleep. Always telling you what you have to eat. Dumpin' turnips on your plate, telling you you *know* they're good when you've known your whole life turnips ain't no good! Ah, me. (*He has his shirt off. He flexes his muscles.*) Remember me, Pops? I'm Walter Morley. They used to come from miles around for just a *sniff* of me! Who's have thought I'd spend my best years living like a bloody monk?

MARGARET. You're hardly a MONK. Monks don't keep whores*
in the town of Raglan.
WALTER. (*Booming.*) I keep no *whore*, Margaret!
MARGARET. You don't?
WALTER. She is not *kept!*
MARGARET. But she is bloody well *supplemented!*
GRAMPS. Now, Margaret, when he goes to the whore there's no
love involved—
MARGARET. (*Mimicking.*) "No love involved!" Well, if there
isn't, he might as well save the twenty and do it himself! (*The
two men react with shock.*)
GRAMPS. Margaret Morley!
WALTER. Filthy, foul, nasty talk! I demand—
GRAMPS. You ought to watch your tongue—
WALTER. Who the hell—how DARE you—
GRAMPS. Shameful language—
WALTER. Apology! Goddamn it, I demand—
MARGARET. Quiet!! (*We hear the tingling of bells.*) I hear Lily
Agnes coming! (*Lily Agnes enters wearing a simple dress. The
occasion for the dress is Gibson. She carries a worn copy of
"Emily Post's Etiquette." She is delicate and graceful, but she has
a rather wizened little face. Her language is "not quite right" but
her behavior is not exaggerated. She is deadly earnest in all
matters; she never tries to be funny. When she enters, she goes
directly to Margaret. She removes her hat, embraces her mother,
and replaces the hat, speechlessly. This embrace is ceremonial.
Gramps waits until the two have separated.*)
GRAMPS. Good morning, Lily. How are you?
LILY AGNES. I am fine, thank you. I am an island of calm in a
turbulent sea. (*Sensing the atmosphere.*) There's an argument,
isn't there? Are you discussing the woman in Raglan?
MARGARET. Yes, we are.
LILY AGNES. She is very ugly.
WALTER. They're all the same in the dark.
LILY AGNES. You are very coarse.
WALTER. And you are bold as brass!
GRAMPS. And I'm too OLD for these shenanigans!

* Pronounced "hoor"

LILY AGNES. And I'm an island of calm in a turbulent sea.

WALTER. Lily Agnes, I want you to tell me honest. How do you feel about this visitor?

LILY AGNES. (*After a moment.*) Ambivalent.

GRAMPS. Walter, that means—

WALTER. I KNOW what that means! (*Pause.*) Explain that, Lily.

LILY AGNES. A young girl's room is a very private place. It's where I keep my personal belongings. It's where I have my private thoughts. And even though we're not religious here my room is, for me, almost like a chapel. (*Walter begins to interrupt.*) Grampa and I adore each other—but that doesn't mean we could share a room. Nearly every night I sing myself to sleep. And it was Grampa who said, "Lily, you have a very interesting voice, but it is—untrained." And you must remember that Grampa snores and sometimes smells medicinal.

WALTER. The *question*, Lily. How do you feel about this visitor?

LILY AGNES. The question at hand is not the one you posed. The question at hand is one of hospitality.

MARGARET. That's right! That's the point.

LILY AGNES. *Gracious behavior.* (*She pats her book.*) In my old book of Emily Post she says that nothing must be spared the guest. She says he should have a good mattress and both a soft, and a firm pillow. He should have a brand new cake of soap, mouthwash and a good clothes' brush. He should have a light at the head of his bed, and two or three books should be provided. These books should be chosen more to *divert* than to *strain* the reader's attention. He should have an ashtray, a calendar, and a clock that works. In August, even though there are screens, he should have a fly swatter. (*Walter stands, incredulous.*)

WALTER. What a lot of crap! Lily Agnes, for the sake of all those things, are you willing to give up your room?

LILY AGNES. Oh, no! Those things require a generosity of self. I could manage them, with grace, for two or three days. I could manage them with a chip on my shoulder for—a week. I can't manage them at all for the whole summer. (*Pause.*) If there's any way to prevent it, I'd rather not leave my room.

WALTER. (*Banging the table.*) Then you *won't* leave your room!

14

Gibson will sleep down here on the Toronto couch. Is that settled, Margaret?

MARGARET. Yes, Walter, it's settled. (*Lily Agnes goes to Margaret. She removes her hat and they embrace again. Implicit in the embrace is Lily's apology.*)

LILY AGNES. I'm sorry.

MARGARET. It's all right, baby. It's all right.

GRAMPS. Lily Agnes, c'mere. Gibson's expected any moment now, and there's something I want to talk to you about.

LILY AGNES. Yes, Grampa. (*She moves to Gramps; they have a quiet, intimate tête à tête.*)

LILY AGNES. What is it?

GRAMPS. Well, Lily, we all know how very fond you are of your hat. We're used to it, you know, in the family. The way you never take it off all day long. But in line with what we were just saying about good manners and all, and what with having a guest in our midst, it really would be nice if you'd take it off at table. (*Lily Agnes frowns and looks to Margaret for an opinion. Margaret averts her eyes.*) I mean, it's perfectly all right the rest of the time. Seems like just some sort of a *quirk*, the rest of the time. But it isn't all right, Lily, at table.

LILY AGNES. We are concerned about Gibson's reaction.

GRAMPS. Yes, a little.

LILY AGNES. The impression we will make.

GRAMPS. That's right.

LILY AGNES. He will find my hat offensive at table.

GRAMPS. I'm afraid he will. He'll wonder why we allow it.

LILY AGNES. But he will see, won't he, that I break my bread? I remove pits from my mouth with some facility? I never place my elbows on the surface and I do not talk, or drink, when my mouth is full.

GRAMPS. Yes, Lily, he'll see all that. But, still, he'll—

LILY AGNES. Still, he'll wonder about my hat. (*She sighs.*) This is such a trivial matter. Leave it to me. Let *me* explain about my hat.

GRAMPS. How will you do that?

LILY AGNES. I will say that without it, I am not contained. My thoughts shoot off in all directions. I want to run naked in the

15

wind and talk gibberish. When I don't have it on, I boil over. I'll tell him, simply: my *hat* is *my* lid.

GRAMPS. All right, Lily. He was always a kind man. Let's hope time hasn't changed him. (*Walter approaches Margaret, speaking quietly.*)

WALTER. Margaret, this here visit would be a whole lot less *awkward* if I went to your bedroom at night, and came out of your bedroom in the morning.

MARGARET. Walter Morley, there is no way to *save face* in front of Gibson. There is no way to *hide* a divided house. The man has a *Ph.D.!* He's lived his whole life in *great books,* and goodness knows, great book are *full* of strange arrangements! (*We hear a car pulling up outside.*) Here's the cab! Oh, God, he's coming! (*She runs to the mirror.*) Oh, God, look at me! I wish I could run and hide!

WALTER. Don't you dare! Don't you dare make a spectacle and leave ME to greet him!

GRAMPS. You all right, Lily?

LILY AGNES. I am fine, thank you. I am an island of calm in a—

GRAMPS. Yes, Lily, thank the Lord for that. (*The four of them line up at a window near the door. Walter bends and peeks through the curtain.*)

WALTER. Who's that driving the cab?

GRAMPS. Probably old Ross McCall—

WALTER. Ross McCall's blind as a bat. He wouldn't be driving—

LILY AGNES. Ross McCall has retired and gone to Victoria.

MARGARET. Is he out of the car?

WALTER. He's out—

MARGARET. Can you *see* him?

WALTER. Yep. I can—

MARGARET. Has he *aged,* do you think?

WALTER. Hard to tell—

MARGARET. Can you see his *hair?*

WALTER. Yep—

MARGARET. Is it *grey?*

GRAMPS. Lily Agnes, what are you doing?

LILY AGNES. I'm afraid I'm quaking.

GRAMPS. Hold onto your hat, Lily! Hold onto your hat. Open the door, Margaret! Open the door! (*Margaret opens the door.*

Gibson stands on the back porch with a large suitcase, a carton of books, and a large brown grocery bag. Margaret embraces him.)
MARGARET. Gibson! Oh, how wonderful you're here! How good to see you! We've all been so anxious! Come in, come in. You must be exhausted. How was the trip?
GIBSON. Oh, fine, thank you. Remarkably free of . . . incident—
MARGARET. You remember Walter?
GIBSON. I do. Indeed I do. *(Shaking hands.)* Good to see you again, Walter.
WALTER. Nice to have you, Gibson.
GIBSON. *(Hugging Gramps.)* And Pops! Hello, hello! Oh, you're *amazing!* You're as dapper as ever. God, what a sight you are!!
MARGARET. And our daughter, Lily Agnes.
GIBSON. Lily Agnes! *(Pause.)* Why, Lily, you remind me of your mother, twenty years ago!
LILY AGNES. That's a lovely compliment, Gibson. But I'm afraid you're mistaken. My true mother was a water witch.
GIBSON. I beg your pardon? *(There is a deadly silence. Walter moves.)*
WALTER. Here—now—let me take your coat and your grip—
GIBSON. Oh, please, don't bother—
WALTER. No bother at all! All in the line of gracious behavior. I'll just sit it here by the Toronto couch—where you're going to sleep—
GRAMPS. *(Lifting the carton.)* Oh, Gibson, this is *heavy!*
GIBSON. Yes, it's books. I'm afraid I have a very lengthy paper to write this summer. *(He sees Walter, going for the bag.)* Oh, but leave the bag. I need the bag. I have gifts!
GRAMPS. Now, Gibson, there was no need for that.
GIBSON. Oh, yes, there *was.* I had a wonderful time looking for gifts. *(His mood begins to change.)* I seldom have a chance to GIVE gifts. *(Pause.)* You are, after all, the only family I've got. *(Pause.)* Whatever . . . small sense of . . . *normalcy* I might have, I know I got from . . . growing up with . . . Margaret. *(He is near tears. He goes to Margaret and hugs her fiercely.)* Oh, Margaret, God help us! So much time.
MARGARET. Yes, Gibson. So much time.
GIBSON. *Cruel* time.

MARGARET. Yes! God, yes.

WALTER. Uh, now, we don't want to start off this visit being *maudlin*.

GIBSON. No, Walter, we don't. You're absolutely right. I think this would be a good time for me to—uh—distribute my largesse. (*Finding the bag.*) I hope you'll forgive this bag. I've never been much good at . . . externals. You know, I was carrying this thing on the plane, and it occurred to me that much could be said for the brown paper bag. I'm surprised it hasn't been done by one of these new, utilitarian poets. Listing it all—you know? The contents. In rhyme. "Ode to a Brown Paper Bag." Well, Well, now. (*He takes out a wad of crumpled tissue paper.*) This is for Margaret.

MARGARET. Oh, Gibson, thank you!

GIBSON. (*As she wades into it.*) Rather too much tissue paper, I'm afraid. (*Pause.*) More of a—*shroud* than a wrap!

MARGARET. (*Taking out a brooch.*) Oh, look at it! It's lovely.

GIBSON. It's the Aztec calendar, Margaret, in copper. I wanted something depicting time, you know? Lost time. Irretrievable time.

MARGARET. Cruel time—

GIBSON. *Finite* time—

WALTER. Now, now, now—

MARGARET. It's truly beautiful, Gibson.

GIBSON. Thank you. Now, for Lily Agnes! I hope your mother won't mind the extravagance of this. I wanted to give you your first handbag. (*He hands her a small alligator bag.*)

LILY AGNES. Oh! Did some poor reptile die for this?

GIBSON. Well, yes, it's alligator—

LILY AGNES. (*Opening it, needing something nice to say.*) The inside's even prettier. Red satin. Thank you very much.

GIBSON. You're very, very welcome. Now, for Walter. I know how busy you are, Walter, with your acres of wheat. I thought you might like to get your mind off the—*terra firma*—now and then. So here is a book. "British Naval Battles, World War II."

WALTER. (*Taking it.*) That's mighty thoughtful of you, Gibson. Thank you.

GIBSON. (*Watching Walter hold the book, awkwardly.*) It can be read, you know, in, uh, increments. Battle by battle. Without, uh, losing the thread. So that one need not concentrate too long if one's attention span is . . . Well, now, let's see. Here we have a gift for Pops. A tricky little piece of equipment—a folding cane! Da-Da!! (*He opens it with a flourish.*) Isn't that ingenious? All these little hinges and screws? And you just fold it up and put it in your pocket. (*He can't get it closed.*) Oh, dear. Oh, well. Perhaps it needs oil or something.

GRAMPS. Thank you, Gibson. You really shouldn't have spent so much money.

GIBSON. Nonsense! You must let me do *something*, Pops. You know, so many times I've awakened in the night and realized I've never thanked you. My God, what *you* did for *me!* It's incalculable. (*To Lily Agnes.*) I was orphaned when I was eight, Lily. And Pops took me in and gave me shelter. And put up with me! I was so miserable, wasn't I, Margaret? So lonely—

WALTER. Well, now, I don't think we want to get into that.

GIBSON. No. Goodness, no, we don't! (*Transition.*) There *is* a little speech I must make. Really, I must, because I've come uninvited—

MARGARET. Gibson McFarland!

GIBSON. I have to warn you, Margaret. I haven't been well. Actually, I've been quite under the weather for sometime now—

MARGARET. You've seen a doctor?

GIBSON. A psychiatrist.

WALTER. Oh, my.

GIBSON. Oh, don't worry, Walter, I'm not bonkers! I seem to be having a crisis of confidence. My work has become . . . meaningless. I don't know why I teach, or why I teach Pope. (*To Walter.*) Alexander Pope?

WALTER. Oh, yes.

GIBSON. I stand at the lectern and face, sometimes, two hundred kids. Half the girls are pregnant—no one listens—they walk around in a stupor—they hallucinate right in front of me and, of course, most of them can't *read*. At the end of each day I go home and turn on the T.V. news. I see riots everywhere, burning, looting, striking. I grieve—I do—I grieve for what we're doing to the Indians and the Eskimos. (*Walter grunts at these references.*) Walter, am I holding things up? Do you have to feed a chicken or something?

WALTER. Oh, no, go on. Please, go on.

GIBSON. Well, for Chrissake, these reporters give you the *names* of the whole damned Mafia! They tell you where they eat. They give you their addresses. Why the hell can't the police find them? And in the midst of all this, I stand at the lectern trying to convince these zonked out kids that Alexander Pope is worth their time! I stand there, a good, industrious, Presbyterian prairie boy, ranting about the genius of a man who was trampled by a mad cow in seventeen hundred and two! A month ago, a young man rose before me, and you know what he said? He said, "Professor McFarland, Alexander Pope is irrelevant in the Twentieth Century." (*Pause.*) Oh, Margaret! Darling Margaret. Thank you for letting me come to your farm. (*He sways and falls to the floor in a dead faint.*)

MARGARET. Oh, Gibson, poor Gibson, my God—

WALTER. It's the airplane! The altitude! Causes fits. (*He runs to the cupboard.*)

MARGARET. Dad—help me! Let's put him on the couch. Gibson, easy now, easy now—

GRAMPS. It's O.K., Lily. Hold onto your hat—

MARGARET. NOW do you understand? *Weltschmerz.* (*Walter comes running with a large soup spoon.*) What in the world is THAT?

WALTER. It's a FIT! He's going to swallow his tongue!

MARGARET. Oh, you fool! It's not a FIT. Go away, Walter, go away!

GIBSON. (*Mumbling.*) They snort it, they sniff it, they cook it, they eat it. . . .

WALTER. I'm TELLING you, he's going to foam at the mouth!

GRAMPS. Get away, Walter! Move your bulk out of here—

WALTER. For God's sake, Margaret, the man's got *mental* trouble!

MARGARET. Gibson? Can you hear me? You're home now, you're safe. We're strong here, all of us, we'll heal you. (*She fusses over him, loosening his tie, removing his shoes.*) There my lad, that's it, stretch out.

GIBSON. Margaret . . . I need . . . Margaret . . .

MARGARET. Yes, you do! And good clear air, and good clean water, and crisp, fresh vegetables out of the garden. And we'll go

off in the woods, the way we used to, and pick pin cherries and Saskatoons and chokecherries. And in no time at all, you'll be restored. (*Stroking his brow.*) Now rest, Gibson. Rest. (*The lights dim on the set. After a moment, they rise on Jake and Archie.*)
ARCHIE. Well, did you get a look at him?
JAKE. I did.
ARCHIE. You took over a keg of fig wine—
JAKE. I took over a keg of fig wine. I walked into the kitchen and I said, "Margaret, me and Archie want to donate a keg of fig wine in honor of Gibson's coming." And he was there, and she introduced us.
ARCHIE. What'd she say?
JAKE. She said Jake and Archie are good neighbors.
ARCHIE. Bless her heart. What's he look like?
JAKE. Well, not bad. Not *bad*.
ARCHIE. Pretty good?
JAKE. Not bad. Walter says there's mental problems, but I couldn't see no trace of it.
ARCHIE. Was he wearing a Vancouver suit?
JAKE. Not when I seen him. He was wearing what city folks consider country clothes. What they call "casual" in the newspaper ads. A hundred dollars, collar to cuffs.
ARCHIE. So what's he doing? Not lifting a hand with the work, I'd imagine.
JAKE. Margaret says he's orienting.
ARCHIE. Orienting?
JAKE. She says he's very busy orienting. First, of course, to the prairie.
ARCHIE. And how's Walter taking it?
JAKE. Walter was down at the compost heap. I said, "Walter, how're you taking this visitor?" Walter said this: He said, "Jake, visitors is *always* a pleasure. If not in the coming, in the going."
(*Lights off Jake and Archie. The lights come up on Gibson, near the Toronto couch. He is alone, in reverie, dressed as described by Jake. It is early morning. Possibly he gazes out of a window.*)
GIBSON. I remember, I remember. The wheat and the barley and oats. The sweet smell of alfalfa. Walking with Margaret in spring, picking the wild mauve crocus. We were two green saplings, dreaming of the world. (*He smiles.*) She was flat-chested,

21

and I had two whiskers—here—and the question was: what would we be? Where would we go and what would we be? We pondered that for three whole summers. Oh, dear God. I'd like to have those summers back again. (*Margaret enters, from her room. She is on the verge of tears, unable to look at him. She busies herself at the stove.*)

MARGARET. Good morning.

GIBSON. Good morning, Margaret.

MARGARET. How are you?

GIBSON. Oh, fine. I've just been remembering all sorts of old things.

MARGARET. Yes. Me, too.

GIBSON. Margaret, this thing is palpable in the house. Lily's not your child, Walter's in the smokehouse. Please. We have to talk.

MARGARET. (*Resigning herself.*) We'd only been married a year. It was a good year—at least I thought it was. I was so proud of myself—a town girl, coming to this farm. I chopped wood, I hauled water, I made cheese. Everybody thought he'd finally met his match. And then the well went dry.

GIBSON. And he hired a water witch.

MARGARET. (*Gazing out across the porch.*) I never cross that porch without thinking of it. It was noon, and I was going out to fetch him in for lunch. And there she was, in the laundry basket. I said, "Walter, is this yours?" And he said, "Yes, I think it is." And Gibson, she wasn't clean. She was all prickly heat and rashy on her bottom. I brought her in and bathed her—in that dishpan. I called her Lily Agnes. That's what I was going to call my own. I hadn't a diaper in the place, so I bleached old flour sacks and scrubbed them on the board till they were soft. I said, "I'll raise this child, Walter, and I'll love it. But you and I are finished."

GIBSON. *That*, I understand. That reaction. But I can't understand fourteen years!

MARGARET. I can't, either. I don't even try anymore. One night, six months after Lily came, I woke up needing him. I couldn't understand why I'd acted so harsh. I got up and put on my robe and went down to the kitchen. When I got to the porch, a faint doubt came over me. I remembered finding the basket. I remembered thinking if I'd had a knife, I'd have run it right through him. But, I went. Down the path, to the smokehouse. When I got

22

there, I couldn't knock. I was all cold sweat, and my hands shook. God help me, I couldn't knock. And then, as I turned away, I saw him at the window. Oh, God, I'd gone such a great distance, all he had to do was open the door. Something prevented him. He says he's the one who did the wrong—it's up to me to do the forgiving.

GIBSON. My God, the pride in this house is of *Biblical* proportions!

MARGARET. About a year later, I tried again. I got up and put on my robe, but I couldn't even get out of the bedroom. (*Pause.*) There's a little splinter of time, Gibson, when you either resolve something, or you don't. If you don't, the time passes, and the splinter becomes a great big wedge.

GIBSON. You could have left. Packed up and left! You still could.

MARGARET. Not without Lily! And where would I go, with Lily? She's not right, you know. She's never mixed with people. And what about Dad? He couldn't handle the house in town, and Walter welcomed him here. And I have no skill, no way to earn a dollar. (*Angrily.*) How easy to say PACK. LEAVE.

GIBSON. There's something about all this . . . water witches, laundry baskets . . . I don't know. I feel as if I haven't journeyed a mere fifteen hundred miles. I feel as if I've gone back, through the millenia. I think I've gone back to the cave!

MARGARET. Oh, don't go putting on your fancy city airs with me!

GIBSON. I am looking for some bit of *logic.* Some small trace of *reason.* You're telling me—YOU, the most passionate girl I ever knew—you're telling me that you *accept* this?

MARGARET. (*Surprised.*) Was I, Gibson? Passionate?

GIBSON. You know damn well you were! Vital and alive and curious and open—yes! Passionate. What a waste!

MARGARET. Do you remember the night you left for university?

GIBSON. Yes, I do. You came to my room and threw yourself on my bed. And you ranted and raved and cried! You said you felt as if you were losing a brother. (*He smiles.*) And you insisted on a keepsake.

MARGARET. A lock of hair—

GIBSON. Yes! I went away with a bald patch. (*Pause.*) After you left, I found a long brown hair on my pillow. And I wondered

23

if I should go. (*Transition.*) Well, it's a perfect example. The rage, the tears, the romantic gesture. And now you stand here and tell me you're *content* with this life till death do you part?

MARGARET. I am NOT content! But I will NOT go out and knock on that door!

GIBSON. See? It's insane!

MARGARET. *You're* a fine one to talk about sanity! *I've* never been to a psychiatrist, and neither has Walter!

GIBSON. And there's the pity! *That's* why we're all standing here like *neanderthals!*

MARGARET. We're only got this summer, Gibson. I want to *be* with you and talk! About Pope, and Vancouver. I want to look at all our old snapshots, when we were kids. Don't let this spoil it.

GIBSON. Well, apparently I'm of no use to my students. Certainly I'm of no use to myself. How can I be of use to you?

MARGARET. Care for me. Be my close friend.

GIBSON. (*Sighing.*) I'm caught in a vise. I have to be civil to Walter.

MARGARET. (*Defensively.*) What does that mean?

GIBSON. I'm his guest as well as yours. I have to *try* and be objective.

MARGARET. About what? He broke faith!

GIBSON. Yes, but you're both at fault.

MARGARET. *I beg your pardon?*

GIBSON. You've both allowed this thing to go on beyond all reason.

MARGARET. Well, I don't see how you can be my friend if you think I'm at fault!

GIBSON. Don't *twist* it—

MARGARET. *You're* twisting it. You've concluded that I am at fault. And frankly, I don't see how you can talk "objectively" out one side of your mouth when brute prejudice is rolling out the other! Where did you learn that little trick? At the university?

GIBSON. Margaret, you're confusing me. I just want to hear Walter's side of the story.

MARGARET. Gibson McFarland, a true friend would see there is only *one* side to this story. Mine. (*She exits to her room, weeping. Gibson slumps down, in a chair.*)

GIBSON. Oh, my God. Wherever I go, I find too much life. (*Walter enters, returning from morning milking. He looks around the room.*)

WALTER. Well sir, it don't look to me like there's gonna be breakfast.

GIBSON. Margaret's upstairs.

WALTER. (*Listening.*) Crying.

GIBSON. Yes.

WALTER. Funny, she ain't cried in years. (*Pause.*) I've got a feeling you've just been given an earful.

GIBSON. How do you stand it, Walter?

WALTER. Now, Gibson, I don't want you getting all upset again. We've lived with this thing for a long, long time. It ain't no picnic, but it's no cause for . . . mental trouble, either. (*Gibson, bewildered, shakes his head.*)

GIBSON. Why do you stay?

WALTER. You gotta understand about the land, Gibson. My Grandad homesteaded here, y'know, and it's come down the line. Five hundred acres. Wherever I put my foot down over five hundred acres, it's mine. It behaves for me. It *performs* for me. And if it don't, I give it a rest. I let it lie fallow a season. Then it comes back and gives me thirty bushels to the acre! (*Pause.*) And the nice thing is, it don't really matter a good goddamn what goes on in this house. Babies been miscarried here. My two brothers died here, an hour apart, from the Scarlet Fever. My Mom. My Dad. Margaret come here as a bride. Lily Agnes come in a laundry basket. (*He hears Margaret weeping, quietly.*) The women cry, but the land just goes on, year after year. Nothin' but death's gonna drive me off this land.

GIBSON. Walter, what is the distance from the smokehouse to that door? A hundred yards? Two hundred?

WALTER. You might as well ask me the distance of the Atlantic Ocean. Gibson, I'm the one who done wrong. It's up to her to do the forgiving. Jesus, man, I tried! I come into this kitchen and pitched in with the heavy work—damn near wore an apron. I sent flowers. Well—I picked 'em and put 'em in a vase and made a goddamn *arrangement*. I brought back a lovely bolt of cloth one time, from town. I said, "Here Margaret, you can make some-

25

thing real pretty with this." Know what she made? Dish towels. Whatya think of that?

GIBSON. I think that erring is human, forgiving is divine.

WALTER. Boy-oh-boy, that hits it on the head.

GIBSON. Alexander Pope wrote that, you know.

WALTER. Nah! *Your* Mr. Pope?

GIBSON. Uh huh.

WALTER. I'll be damned. I thought that come from my old neighbor, Jake, down the road. (*Transition. Walter and Gibson laugh. We hear the slam of a door from Margaret, upstairs. Walter and Gibson become furtive and wary. From this point on, Margaret is listening, offstage.*) Listen, Gibson, we're both men. Can we talk man to man?

GIBSON. Of course.

WALTER. You probably remember the way I was in the old days. I'd come into town Saturady night—'member? They used to come from miles around for just a sniff of me.

GIBSON. I remember.

WALTER. Well, I gotta tell you, since you're bound to find out. I haven't spent the last fourteen years living like a bloody *monk.* I go to a woman in Raglan.

GIBSON. A whore?

WALTER. Well, you know, a widow woman that never was a lady.

GIBSON. I understand.

WALTER. You do? Oh, I'm glad. 'Course, there's no *love* involved. I just go, maybe once a month. For relief.

GIBSON. Does Margaret know? (*Margaret storms in.*)

MARGARET. Yes, Margaret knows! Margaret knows, and Walter goes, and Gibson UNDERSTANDS. Isn't that just hunky-dory! Well, let's see if you understand THIS! (*She kicks a cabinet.*)

WALTER. Margaret, for God's sake—

MARGARET. (*Entirely to Gibson.*) I've raised a child that isn't mine! I'm Lily's Mother in *name* only. I'm Walter's wife in *name* only! But what is HE? He's a legend! He goes into the beer parlour and all those old shitkickers hoot at him! Casanova, they call him! Don Juan! A bastard child at home and a whore in town. (*She begins to move away, limping slightlly.*) But you understand that, don't you? Man to man!

26

WALTER. Margaret, your foot—

MARGARET. My foot is perfectly fine! There is nothing wrong now nor has there ever been anything wrong with MY FOOT! (*To Walter.*) Get out of here! I can't bear the sight of you! Really, I could *vomit!* (*Walter runs out. She turns to Gibson.*) And you *understand.* Mister *Professor!* Mister *Ph.D.!* You're no better than he is. You both wear your brains in your pants! (*She starts to exit, limping.*)

GIBSON. Margaret, are you all right?

MARGARET. (*As she goes.*) I am fine, thank you. I've spent fourteen years living like a bloody NUN, but I am perfectly fine, thank you! (*A moment passes. Gibson runs his hands through his hair and groans. Gramps enters, dressed, from the parlor. He carries the gift cane horizontally in front of him, like a fixed bayonet. He is disgruntled.*)

GRAMPS. Gibson, I can't do *sweet-bugger-all* with this cane!

GIBSON. I'm sorry.

GRAMPS. Y'see? It's *paralyzed.* I don't suppose there were directions?

GIBSON. No, I'm sorry.

GRAMPS. (*Looking around.*) No breakfast.

GIBSON. No.

GRAMPS. And a good deal of weeping and hollering.

GIBSON. Yes.

GRAMPS. You must feel like you've stepped in a can of worms.

GIBSON. Dante's Inferno.

GRAMPS. That, too, probably.

GIBSON. (*Banging a counter.*) Sonofabitch!

GRAMPS. Do you mean life's a sonofabitch, or Walter's a sonofabitch?

GIBSON. I don't know. I'm trying to be *objective.*

GRAMPS. Well, that'll get you nowhere.

GIBSON. What do you mean?

GRAMPS. If something doesn't break this stalemate, the whole lot of us are going to break out in shingles. Now, look. She's my daughter, so I can say it. She's bullheaded. She's loaded with pent-up feelings and she's got no one to share them with. You're like a breath of fresh air, Gibson. You two ought to get out of here. Go out in the woods and pick some berries.

27

GIBSON. (*Reflectively.*) Pops, it can't be easy for you, living here.

GRAMPS. Well, the house in town got too much for me. Weeding the garden, mowing the lawn, shovelling myself out in the wintertime. What's a man to do? (*He sighs.*) It's no bed of roses, but it's better than a little cubicle in the Old Folks' Home. Help us, Gibson. Lend her an ear.

GIBSON. I will.

GRAMPS. Good! Thank you. (*Referring to the cane.*) I'll take this out to Walter. Walter understands these things. (*As he goes.*) Shit, I might as well *use* it! (*He exits to the porch, using his cane. As he leaves the porch, we hear the following exchange.*) 'Morning, Lily Agnes!

LILY AGNES. 'Morning!

GRAMPS. You all done with the separating?

LILY AGNES. Yep. (*Gibson is slumped in a chair. He does not see Lily Agnes cross the porch, and enter. She sees that he is deeply preoccupied. She puts a pail down, and waits a moment.*) I've been waiting to explain about my hat.

GIBSON. Oh, Lily! Good morning. Yes, come tell me all about your hat.

LILY AGNES. We are concerned that you might find it offensive at table. You might think there's been an omission in my training.

GIBSON. Oh, no, Lily. I know your mother's trained you very well.

LILY AGNES. The woman I *call* my mother.

GIBSON. Yes. Right.

LILY AGNES. When I don't have my hat, I'm not controlled. I boil over. I want to run naked in the wind and talk gibberish. When I have it on, all of my instincts are contained. You see? My hat is my lid.

GIBSON. Oh, Lily, I wish I had one. They should hand them out in hospitals, at birth.

LILY AGNES. I'm very anxious to hear about your Alexander Pope.

GIBSON. (*Very happily.*) Are you? Boy, I'd *love* to talk about Alexander Pope.

LILY AGNES. I heard you telling mother about him. Four foot six inches tall, you say, with curvature of the spine. And Roman

28

Catholic to boot, so he had to live ten miles outside London. And corsets, like manacles, to keep him vertical! And three layers of stockings to hide his skinny legs. (*Long pause.*) Now THERE'S a man who needed a hat!

GIBSON. Exactly! But he didn't have one. He only had the paper, Lily, and the pain. (*An idea.*) Listen. This has always seemed to me quite *pivotal*. (*He takes her hand. They walk around the table as he recites.*)

> Why did I write? What sin to me unknown
> Dipped me in ink, my parent's, or my own?
> As yet a child, nor yet a fool to fame,
> I lisped in numbers, for the numbers came
> I left no calling for this idle trade
> No duty broke, no father disobeyed
> The Muse but served to ease some friend, not wife
> To help me through this long disease, my life.*

LILY AGNES. (*Very moved; near tears.*) Oh, dear. This long disease, my life?

GIBSON. Yes. This long disease, my life. (*They reach for each other's hands, and pat each other's hands, as they commiserate, silently, over this line.*)

LILY AGNES. Gibson, have you heard both sides of the story now?

GIBSON. Yes, I think so. I'm trying very hard to be objective.

LILY AGNES. They do need a solution.

GIBSON. Yes.

LILY AGNES. I have to tell you something. (*She looks around, furtively.*) May I rely on your discretion?

GIBSON. Certainly. Do you have a solution?

LILY AGNES. Oh, no. I leave solutions to the adults. I have . . . information. My view, from where I sit. (*Pause.*) I'm very fond of my father, but he's out of the house most of the day and he's in the smokehouse at night. So, I, because I'm kept at home, I keep very close company with my mother. And Gibson, my mother—the woman I *call* my mother—has suffered most. Take heed, Gibson. That is the *truth*. And it comes direct from the source of the trouble. (*She moves away, quickly.*) I've got to go

* "Epistle to Dr. Arbuthnot": Alexander Pope.

29

gather eggs. (*Pause, she sees how weary he is.*) Are you all right?

GIBSON. I don't know.

LILY AGNES. You're not going to faint?

GIBSON. Oh, no.

LILY AGNES. May I ask, how are your accommodations?

GIBSON. Fine, thank you. Very nice.

LILY AGNES. Would you be happier in a private room?

GIBSON. Oh, no. The Toronto couch is just fine.

LILY AGNES. Good! (*As she goes.*) You're picking berries this afternoon?

GIBSON. Yes.

LILY AGNES.   (*Whispering.*) Don't be objective, Gibson! Put sympathy where it belongs! (*She exits, to the yard.*)

CURTAIN

ACT TWO

Three days later. It is afternoon, the kitchen. Gibson sits at the table, which is strewn with books. He is concentrating on Margaret. Margaret thinks he is deep in thought, working. She has peeled onions and potatoes and is presently peeling carrots. She pauses, and looks at Gibson.

MARGARET. You're preoccupied, aren't you?

GIBSON. Yes.

MARGARET. (*Dreamily.*) "The world of the mind." You live in the world of the mind, Gibson. What are you thinking right now?

GIBSON. I'm thinking how beautifully you use your hands. It's . . . lovely to watch.

MARGARET. Oh, Gibson, my hands are a mess! All stained from beets and berries. I thought you were thinking something very lofty.

GIBSON. Oh, but I was! (*He shifts, awkwardly.*) Margaret, some of the farmers around here are very attractive men. Surely they must have made advances, over the years.

MARGARET. Yes, they have. One or two of them. Actually, over the years, three or four.

GIBSON. And you declined.

MARGARET. Yes. You see, they all live here. I mean, they would continue to live here, afterwards. And they all gather in town and talk their heads off. And on top of that, they're all just like Walter. Plain, you know. Not deep. No ideas. So you know right off that . . . in lovemaking . . . they wouldn't be very . . . adventuresome.

GIBSON. (*Smiling.*) I see. Nose to nose and toes to toes.

MARGARET. (*Embarrassed giggle.*) Yes! Oh, my, yes. Exactly! (*She moves to the stove.*) Well, there. That's done. I thought I'd make a nice old fashioned Mulligan stew. It's Jake and Archie's favorite.

31

GIBSON. What time are they coming?

MARGARET. Eight o'clock. They eat so poorly over there, I always try to give them something good. (*Pause.*) Gibson, tell me about your award.

GIBSON. Oh, it's the Governor General's award. They give it every year. I got it for my last book on Pope.

MARGARET. What an honor! Lord, it must be so satisfying, earning your living with your mind.

GIBSON. It's not such a good living, at the university. Luckily, though, there are royalties.

MARGARET. Royalties! What a purple sounding sort of word.

GIBSON. Yes. And I consult quite often.

MARGARET. People consult you—for your *ideas.*

GIBSON. Colleges—boards of education. I advise them on what they ought to include in the curriculum. (*Shyly.*) Two hundred dollars a day.

MARGARET. My God, that's sinful!

GIBSON. Thank you. And sometimes I'm invited to Ottawa. To advise at the Federal level.

MARGARET. The Federal level.

GIBSON. Yes.

MARGARET. The very top.

GIBSON. Yes. (*Pause.*) Margaret, tell me about Daisy's calf.

MARGARET. Daisy's calf?

GIBSON. Yes. I was looking at it in the barn yesterday, and Lily Agnes told me it owed its life to you. Did you nurse it to health or something?

MARGARET. I delivered it.

GIBSON. Tell me!

MARGARET. Well, it was a breech. You know? Daisy was in heavy labor and we were looking for the calf's head, and we couldn't see it. And Daisy was in terrible pain—the noise was awful—and then we saw the calf was coming upside down. We saw the legs.

GIBSON. That's bad.

MARGARET. Very bad. The calf had to be turned, head first. So that Daisy wouldn't be damaged.

GIBSON. Oh, Lord, how do you do that?

MARGARET. Well, you have to use your hands, of course—

GIBSON. Of course—

MARGARET. And you have to maneuver it around, very carefully. And then when you get it in the right position, head first, Daisy does the rest.

GIBSON. My, my, my. (*There is an awkward pause, full of longing and appreciation.*) Well. Shall we to the berry patch?

MARGARET. Yes. Let's clean this off. (*She begins to remove books from the table.*)

GIBSON. I'm in the way here, aren't I?

MARGARET. Not in the least! I *love* having books in the kitchen. I mean, *great* books. All we ever have is Zane Grey. (*She touches the books, fondly.*) Milton . . . Dryden . . . Swift . . . Pope—

GIBSON. Always Pope.

MARGARET. But what's this? Oh, Gibson! (*Incredulously.*) *Palmistry?*

GIBSON. (*Laughing.*) Yes! I've been studying it. It's a sort of therapeutic hobby. My psychiatrist said I had to get away from books and find some mode of *recreation*. This is my recreation: another book.

MARGARET. Can you actually *read* palms?

GIBSON. Yes, I actually can! Well—to be perfectly honest, I have to wing it a bit. But,—wanna try?

MARGARET. (*Very excited.*) Oh, I'd love to!

GIBSON. Come on—over here. (*He takes Maragret and sits her on a high kitchen stool. He stands in front of her.*) Your hand, Madam. Now. All of the mystery, and all of the answers, lie in the seven mounds of the hand. And in the middle, we have a nice big "M," for Margaret! Now, this mound, the heel of the hand, is Mars. That is for courage. Which led you out of Raglan years ago, into these difficult, deprived surroundings. The mound under the little finger is Mercury, for science. Uh . . . these would be the skills you learned in order to survive—agriculture, animal husbandry. The mound at the base of the little finger is Saturn, for fate. (*Pause.*) Lily Agnes calls you mother, but Lily Agnes is not your child. At the base of the index finger is Jupiter, for pride. Oh, my! This mound is very large! It has made a travesty of your marriage these fourteen years. And at the top of the wrist is Luna—imagination. (*Pause.*) I think this means that you and I, out there in the berry patch, have let our minds wander, rather a lot. (*Avoiding her eyes, now.*) Below the thumb is Venus. Which is love. Which is . . . presently quivering.

MARGARET. And the ring finger. What is that?

GIBSON. That is Apollo. The pursuit of art. (*To himself.*) Great books. (*Pause.*) And that, I think, is me. But here's the rub.

MARGARET. Yes?

GIBSON. The finger already bears a ring.

MARGARET. The ring is a travesty. I'll take it off. (*She begins to do so. Gibson stays her hand.*)

GIBSON. No, *I* will take it off. (*He frowns.*) Or, I *would.* If I weren't—

MARGARET. If you weren't—

GIBSON. A good, industrious, Presbyterian prairie boy. (*He moves away.*) Christ, let's get out of here! (*Margaret finds two jam pails, with cord attached. She puts one on, around her neck. She takes the other and holds the cord, reaching up to put it around Gibson's neck. He takes it from her, rather abruptly.*) Oh, please, lady! Have mercy. (*He puts the pail on, and exits, with Margaret following slowly. Blackout. The lights rise on Jake and Archie. They are drinking tea.*)

ARCHIE. Oh, Jake, I must say, you make a good *cuppa.*

JAKE. Thank you, Archie. (*He settles back. lighting his pipe, gauging Archie's mood.*) It's getting thick over there, isn't it?

ARCHIE. Aye, thick. He's classy, isn't he?

JAKE. Oh, yes. He's a artichoke.

ARCHIE. A what?

JAKE. A *artichoke.*

ARCHIE. What's that?

JAKE. Well, it's a very eccentric vegetable. Not one of your more *essential* foods. It takes forever to get to its heart. I saw a bunch of farmers once, didn't know how to eat artichokes. Just didn't have the *patience.* So they devoured 'em, whole.

ARCHIE. Do they eat 'em in Vancouver?

JAKE. I expect so.

ARCHIE. And in Montreal?

JAKE. Oh, yes.

ARCHIE. They'll eat most anything in Montreal.

JAKE. I can see from Margaret's eyes, we're all turnips, and he's a artichoke.

ARCHIE. So there's an attraction taking place.

JAKE. Definitely.

ARCHIE. (*Knitting is brow.*) Of course, what it comes down to, is logistics. He don't have a private room.

JAKE. No. But she does.

ARCHIE. Next to Lily Agnes. That's the fly in the ointment.

JAKE. What about Walter? Dontcha think Walter's the fly in the ointment?

ARCHIE. He's out in the smokehouse.

JAKE. Yep. Well, with Walter in the smokehouse, and Lily Agnes and Grampa in the upper regions, you're left with the Toronto couch, in the kitchen.

ARCHIE. (*After a moment.*) Awful narrow. But, I suppose, where there's a will . . . what about him, for his part? Do you think he's willing?

JAKE. Oh, yes. I think all his parts is willing.

ARCHIE. Then we come to the question: is he *able*?

JAKE. (*Leaning back, expansively, in his chair.*) Archie, don't be influenced by appearances. Education—book learning—don't necessarily act like saltpeter. I know that because I read the book reviews on Sunday. It's the "published letters," you know—the letters of the men who write the books. That's where you catch 'em with their pants down.

ARCHIE. Tell me. (*Avidly.*) Tell me!

JAKE. Well, take our own Bobby Burns, for instance. Did you know *he* sired thirty-six illegitimate children, in between stanzas? (*Archie makes appropriate noises.*) And Lord Byron! There was a rake. Pursued his *sister*, you know, and then bedded down half of London. And, he managed all that with a *club foot!* And then there's a whole horde of Englishmen who did bad things with the Palace Guards. And I shouldn't forget the Frenchman, Balzac. Obese, he was, with a terrible desire for old women. Some people say that poor old Balzac was trying to *recover* his *mother*.

ARCHIE. (*Astounded.*) Imagine that! I wouldn't want to do that!

JAKE. Well, I could go *on* and *on*. Another Englishman, D. H. Lawrence. I read somewheres he said: "Man comes from the womb, and spends the rest of his life trying to get back into it."

ARCHIE. What a dirty thing to say! Listen, I'm anxious to go. What time are we due?

JAKE. Eight o'clock.

ARCHIE. That sounds *formal*. Ties, you think?

JAKE. Wouldn't hurt. And, I'd suggest—a bath.

ARCHIE. Really? You think it's advisable?

JAKE. Oh, yes. After a certain number of days have lapsed, it's always advisable. (*Blackout. Lights up on the kitchen. Gramps wears an apron. He is setting the table. Walter paces. Both are irritable. Lily Agnes sits to one side, studying Emily Post.*)

GRAMPS. Where the hell *are* they? I've made the salad, I'm setting the table. I don't like this. What do you think?

WALTER. I'll tell you what I think. I think you're here making salad, and she's out there, making whoopee.

GRAMPS. (*Seriously, and aware of Lily Agnes.*) You really think so?

WALTER. I do.

GRAMPS. (*Going over to Walter, earnestly.*) Now, Walter, you're not talking to an altogether *inexperienced* man. There's a lot of mileage on this face—these eyes have seen some things I wouldn't dare relate to no one. (*He gazes off.*) Especially that time in Chinatown, when I went to San Francisco. Whew! (*He sighs.*) Oh, my. Through it all, Walter, through all my three score and ten, I've developed *one little kernel* of wisdom. (*He waits.*) One little—

WALTER. Yeah, yeah, what?

GRAMPS. Walter, there's your ordinary whoopee, and then again, there's *whoopee*. It's your farm, damnit. It's your wife. You better hurry up and define just what kind of whoopee's going on!

WALTER. I mean to. I mean to! (*Margaret and Gibson enter. Margaret is angry and frustrated. She bangs down her berry pail and immediately busies herself around the table and stove. After Gramps and Walter comprehend Margaret's mood they turn, simultaneously, to Gibson, and wait for an explanation.*)

GIBSON. Margaret and I were out in the berry patch.

WALTER and GRAMPS. Uh huh?

GIBSON. So many berries out there.

WALTER and GRAMPS. Uh huh.

GIBSON. We lost track of the time. (*Walter and Gramps continue to stare at him.*) And then I saw the sun beginning to set, and I remembered that Jake and Archie were coming. So, we, uh, apologize for being late.

LILY AGNES. Gibson, you haven't met Jake and Archie, have you?

GIBSON. I met Jake, when he brought over the fig wine. I haven't met Archie.

GRAMPS. Well, if you've met one, you've met the other.

LILY AGNES. May I perform the introduction, Mother?

MARGARET. What? Oh, Lily, yes, of course—

LILY AGNES. (*To Gibson.*) Should I introduce you as "Doctor," or "Professor," or—

GIBSON. Oh, Lily, for Chrissake, just *Gibson*. Gibson will be fine.

LILY AGNES. I'd like to know how come all of a sudden everybody's so *crabby*?

GIBSON. I'm sorry. Really, I am. (*Noting her book.*) Are you . . . researching introductions?

LILY AGNES. Yes! Did you know, Emily Post says it's perfectly acceptable to introduce yourself? Yes, you can! If you're left in the lurch at a dinner party. Here's what you're supposed to say. You just sort of—saché over to sombody, and you say: (*She reads, very precisely.*)

"I'm Betsy James. That's my husband sitting opposite you. We live in the country and raise show cattle and dahlias, but we come to town very often in the winter to hear music."

GIBSON. That's very nice, Lily. I'm sure that'll come in handy. (*Turning to Walter.*) What the hell are you looking so sore about?

WALTER. I'm used to my supper being ready at suppertime.

GIBSON. As it has been, you mean, every day for fourteen years.

WALTER. That's what I mean.

GIBSON. And you resent the inconvenience.

WALTER. I do. (*Turning away, abruptly.*) And I don't care to discuss it.

GIBSON. (*To Gramps.*) And you're not happy, either.

GRAMPS. Not right now, no. (*Gramps turns away and sulks.*)

---

* "The Good Conversationalist," Emily Post's *Etiquette*, Funk and Wagnalls, New York.

GIBSON. May I suggest that it is better to register a complaint than to sit and sulk? (*Gramps turns further away.*) Well. This is it in a nutshell, isn't it? The ostrich syndrome. There is a problem. The schedule's been upset. There is tension. So we will all turn our backs, grit our teeth, and hope it goes away. (*He waits a moment. There is no reply.*) Normally, in the course of human events, it becomes clear that communication—that is—the exchange of ideas, will solve almost anything. Normally, it doesn't take fourteen years. (*Again, no response. He begins to pace.*) There is a building in New York City—a noble edifice called the United Nations. When the nations are unhappy they gather, and air grievances, and keep the channels open.

GRAMPS. That's New York City.

WALTER. That ain't here.

GIBSON. Right! But even here we have this magnificent tool. Speech! If we don't use it we might as well be animals. Moose or caribou locking horns until the blood flows.

WALTER. (*To Gramps.*) What the hell is eating him?

GIBSON. I swear to Christ, I'm going to go berserk unless one or two radical changes are made around here. (*To Walter.*) You disappear to the smokehouse. (*To Lily.*) You sit interminably with your Emily Post. (*To Gramps.*) And you, my God, Pops, with your accumulated years and wisdom why haven't *you* made some effort to turn this house around?

GRAMPS. (*Bolting up, taking a stand.*) If there's one damn thing I can't stand, it's criticism! (*He heads for the door, then halts. He stares into the berry pails, and then turns, ominously, to Walter.*) Walter, there's no berries in these pails. (*Walter springs up to look in the pails. All are alert.*)

WALTER. (*Turning to Margaret, ominously.*) Mrs. Morley, there ain't no berries in these pails.

GIBSON. (*Confronting him.*) You're absolutely right, Walter. There are no berries in those pails. I'm the one accountable for that.

WALTER. I ain't talkin' to you! I'm talkin' to my *wife*. (*From this point on he avoids direct eye contact with Gibson.*)

GIBSON. I said I am accountable. We need to talk, Walter.

WALTER. That's just what we're going to do!

MARGARET. Walter, what has to be discussed needn't be discussed in front of Dad and Lily.

WALTER. (*Bellowing.*) Why the hell NOT? I'd be happy to discuss it on the main street of Raglan! I've got nothing to be ashamed of! As far as I'm concerned, the more the merrier! (*Jake and Archie shout from the yard.*)

JAKE. Hey, Morleys, howdy!

MARGARET. Oh, God!

GIBSON. Oh, Jesus!

WALTER. (*At the door.*) Come in, Jake, come in! You're just in time to witness a fine spectacle!

ARCHIE. (*Entering happily, sniffing.*) And I know what it is! Margaret's Mulligan stew. Margaret Morley, you're a *pearl.*

WALTER. Shut up, Archie. Lily Agnes, load up a plate and go to your room!

LILY AGNES. (*Going for a plate.*) But—the introduction!

WALTER. Oh, for Chrissake, hurry up with the introduction. (*Margaret takes the plate.*)

LILY AGNES. Archie, may I say you look very nice this evening? (*She leads him to Gibson.*) I'd like you to meet our guest, Gibson McFarland.

GIBSON. (*Holding out his hand.*) Pleased to meet you, Archie. (*Archie suddenly extends his arms, locks his fingers together and turns his hands inside out so that his two thumbs protrude at the bottom. Gibson is bewildered.*)

LILY AGNES. Gibson, it appears that Archie is doing the farmer's handshake. (*Pause, she whispers:*) When in Rome, Gibson—

GIBSON. Oh, yes. Yes. (*He reaches forward and tugs on Archie's thumbs.*) How do you do, Archie?

ARCHIE. Well, sir, I'm just fine. And I'm delighted—

WALTER. Lily, *git!* Archie— (*He gestures toward Jake.*) get out of the way. (*To Gramps.*) Now, old man, I think you should load up a plate and go to your room.

GRAMPS. I beg your *pardon!* I am three score and ten! I will NOT go to my room! (*Lily Agnes scurries out.*)

WALTER. All right, *stay.* You're a *decent* man—I guess I need all the *decent* men I can get! Move over there. (*He gestures to Jake and Archie.*)

GIBSON. God-*damnit,* Walter! When I first came you said we

could talk, man to man. Now, let's go outside and talk, man to man!

JAKE. (*Whispering, to Archie.*) What's it about?

ARCHIE. (*Turning to Gramps.*) What's it *about*?

GIBSON. It's *about* Margaret and me!

JAKE. Oh, my—

ARCHIE. Oh, dear—

WALTER. (*To Jake and Archie.*) You *heard* it, folks! Remember that! You stood right here in my kitchen and heard it.

JAKE. (*Frightened.*) Walter, we'd like to go home.

ARCHIE. We'd like that very much.

WALTER. Don't you budge a damn inch! *This man* comes here with mental troubles! *This man* takes my wife to the berry patch—

GIBSON. Walter, you're jumping to conclusions! Something has happened here, something has developed between Margaret and me. I want to discuss it. I'm an honorable man—

WALTER. Honorable man! Not a single berry in the pails!

GIBSON. (*To Margaret.*) I swear to Christ, it IS the cave! (*To Walter.*) For once in your life, confront the issues! (*Walter turns, further.*) What kind of chickenshit behavior is this? Turn around and *face* me, *man to man!*

WALTER. (*Pacing, in front of Jake, Archie and Gramps.*) I ain't *talkin'* to that dirty bugger! Since he come to my house, I been denied my own place at table. My food's been thrown down in front of me like slop! Out has come utensils we never used. There's one cracked plate in that cupboard. Big brown crack, right up the middle. Since the Professor arrived, I'm the one who gets that plate! There's a fork in that drawer with two bent tines. I get that, too. I could pick up more with a pair of pliers! (*Pause.*) What I'm watching here is the *chase*. The *kill* is only a matter of time. Archie, ask him! Ask him if he denies that.

JAKE. (*Whispering.*) Close your mouth, Archie. You look like a ninny.

WALTER. ASK HIM!

ARCHIE. Uh, now, Gibson. Do you deny that what's going on here is—the chase?

GIBSON. No, I don't.

WALTER. The *kill*, Jake! *Ask him!*

JAKE. Oh, boy . . . Gibson . . . the kill . . . is that only a matter of time?

MARGARET. (*Throwing a bowl across the room, smashing it, stomping.*) Oh, you BASTARDS!! How dare you! How DARE you gang up on this beautiful man!

WALTER. Beautiful man—

MARGARET. BEAUTIFUL MAN! Do you know what he's done, Walter? He's made me FEEL again. I haven't FELT anything in years. I've walked around here like a bloody machine, going from duty to duty, season to season, like an automated woman. (*Pause.*) I love him. (*Quietly, to Gibson.*) I do, Gibson. I always have. (*Margaret turns and leaves the room. There is a brief, silent moment. Gramps moves to the stove.*)

WALTER. (*Quietly.*) What're you doing?

GRAMPS. I'm too goddamn old for these shenanigans. I'm loading a plate and going to my room. (*He takes a ladle full of stew. Jake and Archie sigh.*) And, Walter, I guess I have to tell you. Whatever transpires here, tomorrow morning I'm gonna have to ride the tide with this daughter of mine. (*He starts to go, stops, and says, pointedly.*) As I have in the past. (*Gramps exits. Walter slowly, sadly, ambles over to Jake and Archie.*)

WALTER. Fellas? Know what we're going to do?

JAKE and ARCHIE. Uh uh.

WALTER. We're going to Raglan.

ARCHIE. For relief?

WALTER. For beer. Lots and lots of beer. And then we're all goin' home to your house. (*Jake and Archie register surprise.*) And I'm gonna stay there, till they're all done with busting their commandments. (*Pause, he looks around the room, confused.*) I'll need clean pyjamas.

ARCHIE. I've got extra.

WALTER. (*Still not facing Gibson.*) When are you leaving my house?

GIBSON. I told the cab man Labor Day.

WALTER. She can expect me back the day after. Just in time for harvest. (*He turns to Gibson.*) This land is *mine*, Gibson. Nothing but death'll drive me off this land. Let's go!! (*Walter, Jake and Archie exit. Margaret enters, sheepishly and vulnerably, with Lily Agnes. Lily wears her nightie, her hat, and carries her book.*)

41

LILY AGNES. I've come to say good night.

GIBSON. Good, Lily, I'm glad you did. (*He glances at Margaret.*) Your father's gone down to Jake and Archie's for awhile.

LILY. Yes. I was just upstairs, trying to find the appropriate passage. It's here, under "Planning Your Trip." I'd hoped to read it to my Dad before he left. (*To Gibson.*) May I read it to you?

MARGARET. Lily—

LILY AGNES. Mother, I think it's important.

GIBSON. Please, go ahead.

LILY AGNES. (*Reading.*)

"If you wish to enjoy your trip to the full, with a minimum of worries, there are several precautions that you must take, to insure the safety and well being of the people you have left behind."

GIBSON. Lily Agnes, all that's left behind is safe with me.

LILY AGNES. Yes, the *things*—

GIBSON. The people, too. What's the matter, Lily?

LILY AGNES. When the time comes for you to plan your own trip, I wonder—*which* of the people you'll leave behind.

GIBSON. You're asking me if I intend to take—

LILY AGNES. My mother. Yes. That's what I'm asking. (*Margaret rushes in, embracing Lily Agnes. Lily removes her hat.*)

MARGARET. Lily, Lily, Lily, what a silly question! What a silly duck you are! Of course, he'll go alone. Did you really have to ask? (*Standing back.*) Look at us! You with your silly hat. And me—so . . . rough. So . . . homespun. We're lumps of prairie turf, you and I. Wouldn't we be a sight, walking down Granville Street? (*She takes Lily by the shoulders, gently.*) Listen. One thing I'm living proof of. I stay. I don't quit. I may rant and rave, but I'm solid. (*She whacks Lily across the rear.*) Run along now, to bed. I think we've settled that.

LILY AGNES. Yes. And to my satisfaction. (*Pause.*) For which I'm very grateful. (*She begins to replace her hat, pauses, and then goes to Gibson. She hugs him.*) Goodnight, Gibson.

GIBSON. Goodnight, Lily. And thank you for that.

LILY AGNES. You're very welcome. I feel very well contained tonight. (*To Margaret.*) For which I'm very grateful. (*Lily Agnes exits. Margaret and Gibson watch her go. Margaret, afraid, and strangely virginal, begins to move around the kitchen.*)

MARGARET. I had a terrible bout of conscience a minute ago, upstairs. I thought, my God, this is happening in Walter's house. But then I wondered, what does a woman have to do to call her house her own? Every nook and cranny of this house has known my hand. I've scrubbed it, polished it, repaired it. I know how it cracks in the sun and moans in the wind. I haven't, for fourteen years, shared it. This house is *mine*. And what will happen in it will happen to *me*. (*Gibson takes a step towards her. She is not ready. She moves to the window.*) There's no moon. And you're wearing denim. I wanted to bathe in lavender a moment ago, but I couldn't find any. (*Turning to him, directly, tearfully.*) My need is awful. It's naked. I can't even dress it up in sweet aromas. I want to be kissed and held. I want to leave my hair on your pillow. (*She holds her arms out to him. He embraces her, kisses her. They part slightly, and Gibson takes off Margaret's wedding ring. She takes it and drops it in a china cup, or bowl. We hear the metal tinkle. Gibson embraces her once more. The lights dim. The lights rise on Jake and Archie's table. They are just finishing their breakfast. We see that a place has been set for Walter. After a moment, Walter enters. He wears Archie's pyjamas, which are too small for him. He is barely able to contain his anger. He stands behind his chair.*)

WALTER. Morning.

JAKE. Morning.

ARCHIE. Cuppa tea?

WALTER. No, thank you. Your water over here makes the tea taste funny. (*Suddenly he picks up his chair and bangs it to the floor with a crash.*) Jee-sus!

JAKE. Easy on the chair, Walter, easy on the chair! Sit down, now, and eat something. (*He half rises, headed for the stove.*)

WALTER. I'm not *going* to eat! I only come out because I can't be alone a minute longer. (*He sighs, settling down in his chair.*) Oh, fellas. Once upon a time I was twenty—

    ARCHIE. So was I.

    JAKE. Me, too.

WALTER. (*He begins playing with the cup which has been set out for him.*) And there was this pretty girl, pure as the driven snow.

JAKE. Margaret—

ARCHIE. From the Greek—

JAKE. A pearl.

WALTER. And her father was Mayor of Raglan. So she *moved,* as they say, "in the right circles." And I sez to myseelf, "This is the one I'll give my name to." (*He bangs the cup in the saucer.*) Well, now I'm forty. (*He bangs again.*) And Mrs. Morley's down the road, wearing the Scarlet A.

ARCHIE. Mind the cup, Walter, mind the cup! We've only three cups in the place.

WALTER. Oh, I'm sorry. I wasn't thinking. (*Archie burps. Walter waits a minute, looking at Archie, incredulously.*) Say excuse me.

ARCHIE. 'Scuse me.

WALTER. That's what happens when there's no woman in the house. When there's no woman in the house, there's no *manners.* (*He picks up a fork and begins to play with it. He looks to the ceiling.*) God grant me the strength to get through this summer.

JAKE. Walter, listen. You have to remember, that farm is *yours.* Your name is on the deed.

WALTER. And what'll THAT be worth when the Professor gets done with it? He don't know sweet-bugger-all about farming.

ARCHIE. Margaret does, though. She'll teach him.

WALTER. *Margaret does?* Ha. Ha. Ha. Lemme tell you about *Margaret.* That first October, when she come fresh to the farm? She set about planting tulip bulbs, for the spring. I seen her out there, making little holes, and I could feel it in my bones, something was haywire. Know what she was doing? (*Jake and Archie nod "No."*) She was planting the bulbs *upside down.* She was putting the knobs—you know—the *corms,* face down. I said, "Margaret, you plant 'em *that* way, they're going to get your tulips down in China!" "Margaret'll teach him." Ha! (*On this last line, he bends the frail, aluminum fork into a "U."*)

JAKE. For Chrissake, Walter! (*He lifts the fork, to show Archie.*) Look at this, Archie! He's ruined our fork!

WALTER. God, I'm sorry. I really am sorry. But you have to understand how painful it is, sitting here knowing my farm is going to ratshit.

ARCHIE. Margaret's been *fifteen years* on that farm—

44

WALTER. Margaret don't know *nothin'!* (*He picks up a spoon and waves it at Archie.*) You remember six years ago, when I cracked all them ribs? I was in the hospital for four days. She forgot the cows need roughage. She left the oats out of the fodder! When I got home she gave me a glass of milk. I'm tellin' you, man, I coulda PISSED a better glass of milk! (*On the last line, he bends the spoon. Archie grabs it.*)

ARCHIE. Goddamnit, Walter, now you've mashed the spoon! Will you lay off the silverware?

WALTER. I've got *no* control! No control, over nothing! My farm, my life, my wife—and I want you to know, Archie, I'm not so crazy about these pyjamas. (*He bangs the table.*) What I'm feeling is *rage.* I want *revenge.* I lie in there and this rage eats away like a termite in my gut. (*Pause, he makes an evil face and uses an evil voice.*) And I find myself making *plans.*

JAKE. Holy Jesus, Walter, what kind of plans?

WALTER. (*Holding the cup again.*) First, I'd make a gelding of him. *Zip, zip,* and he'd sing like a soprano! Then I'd hang him upside down from that big willow tree on the east forty. Then I'd weigh him down heavy with the collected works of Alexander Pope. (*On "Alexander Pope," he breaks the handle off the cup.*)

ARCHIE. *Now* you've done it! You've busted the cup!

WALTER. Oh, I'm sorry! Really, boys—

JAKE. What a damn shame! Now we've only two left.

WALTER. Well, hell, that don't matter. I don't need one. (*Annoyed.*) Your water over here makes the tea taste funny. (*Blackout on Walter, Jake and Archie. The lights rise on the kitchen. It is shortly after breakfast. The table is cluttered with dirty breakfast dishes. Margaret is seated at the table, enjoying a quiet cup of coffee, thinking. Gibson is seen on the porch, leaning against a rail, reading. Margaret finishes her coffee and moves over to the unmade Toronto couch. She stands over it, smiling. As she begins making up the bed, Gibson sticks his head in the door, still holding his book.*)

GIBSON. Darling? I'm getting a little anxious. How soon'll the table be ready?

MARGARET. Oh, soon! Very soon. I just want to pull this together. (*She pats the bed. Gibson looks at the bed. He smiles warmly, and then looks at Margaret with deep feeling.*)

45

GIBSON. Thank you, "passionate woman."

MARGARET. (*Very pleased with herself.*) You're very welcome. (*She goes to the table, to remove the dishes.*) I'll give a holler, when it's ready.

GIBSON. Good. This really is a bitch, having no place to work. (*He goes back to the porch and sits down with his book. Margaret starts to clear the table. Lily Agnes crosses the porch. She is hot and exhausted.*) Hello, Lily.

LILY AGNES. (*Disgruntled.*) Hello, Gibson, hello. (*She enters the kitchen.*)

MARGARET. Lily Agnes, grab some plates. Gibson needs the table. (*Lily Agnes goes to a chair and falls in it.*) Lily, I *said* grab some of these plates! I need help.

LILY AGNES. I just fed the chickens. (*Pause.*) "Gibson's job."

MARGARET. I know, Lily, I know, but he's so preoccupied with this paper he has to write—

LILY AGNES. Two weeks ago I told him if he didn't put grit in the mash mixture, the gizzards would clog up. I told him if he didn't use calcium compound, the eggshells would crack. Did he listen? No. You know what he said? He said he thought chickens were very stupid. He said he didn't understand their *mentality.* I said, "Gibson, they HAVE no mentality." I said that's where we get the term "bird brain." Well, today I went to check. I spotted lice and mites. (*Margaret reacts, covering her mouth.*) Yes, We've got a *spectacular* case of fowl pox in the hen house. (*Gramps comes across the porch, hot and exhausted. He wears boots and overalls.*)

GIBSON. Hello, Pops.

GRAMPS. (*Disgruntled.*) Hello, Gibson, hello. (*He enters, falls in a chair, and groans.*)

MARGARET. What's the matter?

GRAMPS. I ache.

MARGARET. Didn't Gibson help with the milking?

GRAMPS. No, he didn't. He wandered off, on the way to the barn. He said he wanted to contemplate the sunrise. He's done that four mornings in a row, now. Contemplated the sunrise. What I wonder is: how many times does a man have to contemplate the sunrise before he comes to some sort of *conclusion.* (*He notices Margaret picking up two halves of a cast iron skillet. She moves to*

46

put them with the things to be washed.) What happened to the skillet?

MARGARET. It—broke. (*Pause.*) It was—taken right from the hot stove and put in cold water and it—broke.

GRAMPS. (*Exchanging looks with Lily.*) Uh huh. (*He lights a pipe.*) Well, I'm going to rest a minute before I go out and shovel the barn. (*Margaret has cleared and wiped the table. She goes to the door.*)

MARGARET. Gibson? You can work now. The table's ready.

GIBSON. Hurray! (*He enters in a slightly manic state, anxious to put stored-up thoughts down on paper. He carries several books to the table, and distributes two or three pads of paper. Gramps is sitting back, smoking, reading a newspaper. Margaret is ready to wash the dishes.*)

MARGARET. Come on, Lily. Grab a towel. (*Lily Agnes groans.*)

GRAMPS. Go ahead, Lily! Lend a hand.

MARGARET. (*Washing dishes.*) Do you have everything you need, Gibson?

GIBSON. Pardon? Oh. Well, I could use a good library.

LILY AGNES. (*Drying dishes.*) There's a good library in Raglan.

GIBSON. No, no, Lily, all they have is novels. Best sellers. I mean a *library.*

LILY AGNES. Oh. (*A moment passes. Gibson scribbles furiously on a pad. Then, very quietly, Lily Agnes begins to sing. This is common routine in the house—to hum or sing during monotonous work. Singing, drying dishes.*)

 Gin a body meet a body
 Comin' thro' the rye
 Gin a body kiss a body
 Need a body cry?

(*Margaret joins in.*)

 Every lassie has her laddie
 Nane, they say, hae I
 Yet a' the lads they smile at me
 When comin' thro' the rye.

(*A moment passes, then Gramps joins in.*)

 Among the train there is a swain
 I dearly lo'e my sel'
 But whaur his hame, or what his name

47

I dinna care to tell.

(*Gramps, Margaret and Lily Agnes now give a rousing finish to the song. During this last verse Gramps taps the beat with his foot enthusiastically. Gibson, unable to continue, sits mesmerized by Gramps foot.*)

> Every lassie has her laddie
> Nane, they say, hae I
> Yet a' the lads they smile at me
> When comin' thro' the rye.

(*Gibson bolts up and starts collecting the books and papers.*)

MARGARET. Oh, Gibson, I'm *sorry!* Did that disturb your work? (*He refuses to look at her.*) Oh, I'm so sorry! We always find a little song *helps* with the work—

GIBSON. *This* work is not helped by a little song. This work is severely *hindered* by a little song. This *place,* this . . . hub of domesticity, is simply *no good* for serious work!

MARGARET. (*Slapping down a dishrag.*) Well, we have *five hundred* acres here! FIND ANOTHER PLACE! (*Margaret and Gibson stand, riveted, scowling at each other. Gramps puts his paper aside.*)

GRAMPS. Lily Agnes, I think you oughta go do the separating, and I oughta go shovel the barn. (*Lily Agnes puts her towel down and goes to the door, waiting for Gramps. Gramps, passing Gibson.*) Gibson, when you look at me, what do you see?

GIBSON. Are you *serious?*

GRAMPS. Yes! What do you see?

GIBSON. Well . . . a man . . . mellow in years, kind and . . . generous—

GRAMPS. No, no, NO! You see a man, three score and ten, on his way to a morning of shoveling shit. (*Gramps and Lily Agnes exit.*)

MARGARET. Gibson, this is the prairie. There are no great libraries here. We're not the *brains* of the country, we're the *breadbasket.* WHEAT is our business. You may think your work is more important, but answer me this, if you will: What does an army travel on?

GIBSON. Oh, Margaret—

MARGARET. *What does an army travel on?*

GIBSON. (*Resignedly.*) Its belly.

48

MARGARET. Its BELLY! That's where *we're* at, Gibson, the belly of the country. (*Pause.*) We have a system here: we work eight hours, we sleep eight hours, we have eight hours for fun. This paper you have to publish has put you right out of *commission*. You are no *fun*, Gibson.

GIBSON. Will you *stop* this? Will you stop standing there like the Rock of Gibraltar?

MARGARET. The WHAT?

GIBSON. The Rock—

MARGARET. That's an insult!

GIBSON. Listen, I'm not the basket case I was when I arrived! This is the prairie and this is a fight—and I *know* how you fight on the prairie. This is where I *learned*, for Chrissake. You fight DIRTY. So don't pull that "insult" stuff with me!

MARGARET. *My old Dad* is limping around here with lumbago! I haven't spent a single minute with my daughter in a month! I've got livestock wandering around this farm so pitiful it's a wonder we're not *quarantined*.

GIBSON. Ah ha! *Now* we hit pay dirt. You want me to be *both* a scholar of great books *and* a tiller of the soil. Let me tell you something, lady. You can't have it both ways. Even if I didn't have the pressure of this paper, I *still* would hit the books every day. It's my life—my bread and butter—it's just not my *nature* to fart away a whole summer!

MARGARET. You are *saying* that I, and Lily, and Dad, in following our normal routine—you are saying that we *fart away* our summers! Let me tell *you* something, Mr. Professor! You *hide* in books. Books are your security blanket. You *bury* yourself in books to escape reality.

GIBSON. Can I believe my ears? Are you asking me to equate— can I BELIEVE you're asking me to equate *reality* with *shovelling shit?*

MARGARET. Oh, *equate it* however the hell it fits! (*On the verge of tears.*) When you work, a wall goes up around you. You seem, somehow, off limits. It makes me feel very . . . alone. When I talk to you, you don't hear me. Walter always heard me. He was good company. He was in and out of the house, and we shared the work. Oh, Gibson, forgive me. I did want it both ways. Forgive me for being so romantic.

GIBSON. (*After a moment.*) There's really nothing to forgive. I'm the hopeless romantic, Margaret. I thought I'd come out here and you'd all go about your business, and I'd just sort of graft myself onto that and somehow benefit. I imagined myself on the periphery, watching a pastoral dream. (*Pause.*) Now I see all this involvement—all this *coping*. I can't share it, Margaret. I feel like a displaced person.

MARGARET. But Gibson, the prairie's your home. The only home you ever had. How can you feel displaced?

GIBSON. I don't know. This room, this life, Pops and Lily and Walter—the cosy on the teapot. They're all uniquely yours. I was happier on the periphery, Margaret. I'm the one to forgive. (*She goes to him, taking his hand.*)

MARGARET. When you were eight years old, and you came to us, do you know what Dad said? He said, "Margaret, we must be careful with this boy. He has an intimate acquaintance with sorrow."

GIBSON. (*Quietly resigned.*) I guess that's it. The truth of me. It's the thing I don't want to share with anyone. (*Pause.*) I don't want to be known that well.

MARGARET. Would you like to be alone?

GIBSON. No. Would you?

MARGARET. No. (*She sits him down on the Toronto couch, then sits beside him.*) Let's just sit and have a quiet hug. (*They sit, gazing into space. The lights rise on Jake and Archie's table. Walter sits alone, dejectedly, playing solitaire. He still wears Archie's pyjamas. After a moment, Jake and Archie enter, wearing jackets.*)

WALTER. Jesus, you been gone a long time! I thought you'd just go down there and sneak around and check things out for me, and come right back!

JAKE. *We* thought *you* might get dressed.

ARCHIE. It's depressing, Walter, the way you never get dressed.

WALTER. I wanna know what you *saw!*

JAKE. Well, we saw it. But I'm not quite sure we believe it.

WALTER. Tell me!

ARCHIE. Well, we had to hide in the bushes till it got really dark. Then, when it got dark, we snuck up to the house. Lily was all ready for bed and the old man was sitting in his chair with a hot water bottle on his back.

WALTER. Uh *huh*.

JAKE. Then we see there's a light on in the hen house. So we sneak over there—how do they say—*stealthily*. And guess what's happening there?

WALTER. What?

JAKE. Margaret's in there with the disinfectant. Spraying with a hose. So you can conclude from that: you've got fowl pox in the hen house.

WALTER. Oh, Jesus.

ARCHIE. Then we see another light. You'll never guess where.

WALTER. Where?

ARCHIE. The smokehouse.

WALTER. No!

ARCHIE. Yep. So we snuck over there, and *Gibson's* in there with books and a whole lot of that yellow foolscap spread all over your table.

WALTER. He's been banished to the smokehouse! I'm tellin' you, it's a *habit* with that lady!

ARCHIE. No, no, I'm afraid that's not the case. He's using it for a study. Because, well, Margaret finished up the spraying and then she went to the house. So, of course, we snuck back there and watched. (*He is getting squeamish. He looks at Jake.*) Well, she undressed and put on a nightie. I don't know where the hell she got that nightie, but it wasn't, if you know what I mean, it wasn't no *married* kind of a nightie.

WALTER. You dirty buggers! You watched her change?

JAKE. You *sent* us, Walter! You sent us!

WALTER. Get on with it.

ARCHIE. Well, then—this is about eleven o'clock. She mosies on out to the smokehouse.

WALTER. (*Banging the table.*) BITCH!

JAKE. Do you wanna hear this or not?

WALTER. I want to. Go ahead, Archie.

ARCHIE. Well, we snuck over there again and, uh, (*He clears his throat.*)—well, a lot of affection transpired there between the two while Gibson put his books away.

51

WALTER. A lot—

JAKE. A lot. And her in that nightie. After that they came out, and they were chatting, you know, and they walked to the house.

WALTER. Didja *hear* anything?

ARCHIE. Coupla things. Margaret says, "One more week, Gibson, one more week." And he replied something poetical.

WALTER. Do you remember it?

ARCHIE. I do. (*Embarrassed.*) But it was—poetical. (*He adopts classical tones.*) He said, "Ye Gods, annihilate but space and time and make two lovers happy."

WALTER. (*Barely audible.*) I see. Then they went to bed?

JAKE. Yes. We stayed there by the window till the lights went out.

WALTER. (*With a lewd expression.*) Didja *hear* anything?

JAKE. Walter, there are *limits* to what we'll do in the name of friendship!

ARCHIE. I'm surprised you didn't send us down there with the Kodak and the flash bulbs! (*Pause, he groans.*) Make a cuppa tea, Jake, make a cuppa tea.

JAKE. I will.

WALTER. None for me, thanks.

ARCHIE. (*Disgruntled.*) We know, Walter, we know. The water here at our place makes the tea taste funny. (*Blackout. The lights rise on the kitchen. It is shortly before Gibson leaves. We see him, in his city clothes, sitting and polishing his city shoes. Gramps is busy packing the carton of books. Margaret and Lily Agnes are packing Gibson's clothing at the Toronto couch. A moment passes. There is a pervasive sadness.*)

LILY AGNES. You really should have a keepsake.

MARGARET. (*Whispering.*) You know what I'd like?

LILY AGNES. What?

MARGARET. A lock of hair.

LILY AGNES. Ask him! (*Lily Agnes finishes the packing. Margaret goes to Gibson, leans over, and whispers in his ear. He answers sadly.*)

GIBSON. Of course. (*She goes to a cupboard to get scissors, a comb and an envelope. She returns to Gibson and combs through his hair, silently.*) You did this once before.

MARGARET. Yes. The *first* time you left.

GIBSON. Did you lose the other?

MARGARET. No, it's in a locket upstairs. But *this* one'll have a bit of gray.

GIBSON. I see. (*He smiles.*) A *series.* (*She moves away and places the snip of hair in the envelope. He watches her with an ineffable sadness. Pulling himself out of it, he turns to Lily Agnes.*) Well, Lily, what a good job! Thank you very much.

LILY AGNES. You're very welcome.

GIBSON. (*Awkwardly.*) You've been very patient, and very kind.

LILY AGNES. Thank you. You've been very . . . interesting. And Gibson, I think you've also been very beneficial.

GIBSON. I hope so. It's a comfort, when you're fond of people, to serve a purpose. (*Hugging her.*) Try and have a good life, Lily. (*We hear a car motor.*)

MARGARET. Here's the cab! Lily, close the suitcase. Gibson, where's your jacket?

GIBSON. Oh, yes, uh—here it is. Now, uh, where did I put my tickets—

GRAMPS. (*Holding them.*) Absent minded Professor! Here they are. I found them on the porch.

MARGARET. (*Peering out, nervously.*) Let's see who they sent this time—

GRAMPS. (*Peering out.*) Oh, good! It's that fellow, MacDougal—

GIBSON. Oh, that's good—

GRAMPS. Yes, isn't that good? You won't have to make conversation if you don't want to. (*Pause, he turns to Gibson, feebly. He knows he will never see him again.*) Since . . . you've already met him. All set, then?

GIBSON. (*Embracing Gramps.*) Good bye old man. Take care.

GRAMPS. Safe trip, Gibson, safe trip. Can you manage the carton?

GIBSON. Yes, thank you. Lily Agnes—(*He embraces Lily.*) Hold onto your hat, Lily. (*After letting go of Lily, he pauses. He is unable to look at Margaret.*)

MARGARET. I'll come out with you. (*Gibson and Margaret exit to the porch. Gibson carries the carton of books, Margaret, the suitcase. They pause, and are seen, on the porch. We hear the following:*)

GIBSON. (*Offstage, on porch.*)
     Where'er you walk, cool gales shall fan the glade

Trees, where you sit, shall crowd into a shade
Where'er you tread, the blushing flowers shall rise
And all things flourish where you turn your eyes.

(*Gibson leaves the porch. The car motor starts. Margaret enters, slowly. She exchanges looks with Lily Agnes.*)

LILY AGNES. I'm worried about him. (*Margaret nods, "yes."*) Has he always been this lost? (*Margaret is unable to answer. She goes and picks up the envelope, with the lock of hair.*)

GRAMPS. Always. I gave him an address, but that didn't help. He was still lost.

MARGARET. I remember, when we were kids I was reading the whole set of "Anne of Green Gables." Gibson read the darndest things. He was always seeking out books written by exiles. Russians living in England, Germans living in France, Englishmen living in Italy. He said it reinforced him. Made him feel less cut off from his roots. He's a misfit, Lily.

LILY AGNES. Yes, I see that. (*She is on the brink of tears. She begins to whisper:*) I am an island of— (*Gramps rushes to her, to comfort and hug her.*)

GRAMPS. Now, listen, Lily, he's very lucky, as misfits go. His work is acknowledged. He's got many publications, and three degrees. All the things that look good on paper. He's healthy, he's not hungry. His handicap's all in his head. That's not so bad. At least that way people don't gawk and point a finger. Buck up, now, Lily, buck up. (*We see Walter step up on the porch. He is followed by Jake and Archie. Walter places himself in the doorway and waits a moment, hoping that someone will notice him. Margaret, Gramps and Lily Agnes are all deep in thought.*)

WALTER. Margaret?

MARGARET. (*Turning.*) Oh. Hello, Walter. (*She sees Jake and Archie on the porch.*) You needn't have brought your henchmen.

WALTER. (*Nodding.*) Pops.

GRAMPS. Hello, Walter.

WALTER. Lily Agnes.

LILY AGNES. Hello, Dad.

WALTER. (*Faltering.*) I missed you, Lily.

MARGARET. (*Taking command.*) Jake and Archie, if you don't mind, I'd like you to stay out on the porch for a minute. Lily— Dad—I'd like you to join them.

54

GRAMPS AND LILY AGNES. (*Scurrying out.*) Yes. Of course. Fine. (*Walter moves a few steps into the room, surveying it carefully.*)

WALTER. This is—very hard.

MARGARET. Yes.

WALTER. (*Another step or two.*) This sure ain't easy.

MARGARET. No.

WALTER. (*Looking around.*) His soap. His towel. The dishes he ate off. His place at table. (*His eyes rest on the Toronto couch.*) The place where he—you slept. And what's that you're holding?

MARGARET. A lock of his hair.

WALTER. (*A deep, anguished moan.*) Oh, Jesus! (*He turns to leave.*) I don't think I can stay.

MARGARET. Walter, you must. You really must.

WALTER. Why, Margaret, why?

MARGARET. Because I did.

WALTER. I see. (*Pause. He slowly nods his understanding.*) Well, it's a fair enough place to begin. (*Margaret, in a sudden, explosive rage, bangs the counter.*)

MARGARET. Oh, you BASTARD!

WALTER. I beg your PARDON?

MARGARET. If you weren't such a BASTARD this never would have happened! You SAW me in the yard, years ago, trying to knock! I saw YOU, watching me, at the smokehouse window! But YOU wouldn't open the door! No! YOU couldn't meet me half way and reach out and open the door! Not Walter Morley! HIS ARM was paralyzed. He had a GRAND PIANO on his arm! HE'D rather go to a dirty old whore and risk a goddamn social disease! Oh, you really are a— (*Walter goes to her, grabs her, embraces her roughly.*)

WALTER. Margaret, Margaret, Margaret—please! I'm *sorry*, Margaret! I'm sorry for all of it. I'm *so* sorry!

MARGARET. (*Crying.*) I'm sorry, too—*so* sorry—

WALTER. I never said a *word*, never *could*, for the way you've loved Lily—

MARGARET. No need, Walter, no need—

WALTER. Yes, yes, *thank you*. I noticed it all, all the tutoring, all the kindness—

55

MARGARET. No need, Walter, no need. Please. (*They are both crying.*) Goodness! Oh, goodness—

WALTER. Sakes alive, yes. No need to be . . . maudlin—

MARGARET. No, no. Goodness, no. We don't want to be *maudlin.*

WALTER. (*Wiping his eyes, gesturing to the porch.*) We've got a regular town gathering out on the porch.

MARGARET. Yes. I'll get them in. (*On her way, she stops at the cup that holds her ring. She puts the ring on. Walter does not notice. She moves to the door.*) I'm sorry. We had to talk. (*All four: "We understand." "Quite all right." "Don't mind at all," "Not in the least." They enter. Gramps heads for his chair, Lily Agnes removes her hat and embraces Walter.*) Jake, I want to thank you for taking care of my husband.

JAKE. (*With a pained look.*) Our pleasure, Margaret. Our pleasure.

MARGARET. (*Laughing.*) Darned little *pleasure,* I imagine. He's not an "easy keeper." Never has been. (*She moves to the stove.*) And he's worse, I know, when he's idle.

WALTER. Jesus, I'd like a cup of tea! I haven't had a cup of tea in six whole weeks!

MARGARET. Really? (*Glancing at Archie.*) Why is that?

ARCHIE. The water down at our place makes the tea taste funny.

MARGARET. Oh, I see. (*She smiles at Walter.*) Well, I'll put the kettle on. Now, let's see. I have some . . . butter tarts, I think and, uh, half a spongecake. (*Jake and Archie hurry to sit at the table.*)

JAKE. Oh, I always say leftover cake's the best!

ARCHIE. A privilege to be invited, Margaret!

GRAMPS. (*Coming to the table.*) So, fellows, what are you predicting for the crop?

WALTER. (*Sitting down.*) Bad.

JAKE. Bad.

ARCHIE. Terrible.

GRAMPS. You farmers say the same thing every year! Give me a figure. (*Lily Agnes helps Margaret. She puts cream, sugar, etc., on the table.*)

WALTER. I'll give you a figure all right! And it's *bad.* Fifteen measly bushels to the acre!

GRAMPS. Oh, that is bad—

JAKE. We don't reckon it quite that bad, Walter. We're hoping for twenty.

GRAMPS. Well, if *you* get twenty, *we'll* get twenty. The top-soil's all the same. Can't complain about that. Better than last year.

MARGARET. *Last year* we had two hailstorms! The year before that we had smut in the granery.

WALTER. *Next year,* though! Next year they're predicting a bumper! Thirty bushels to the acre!

MARGARET. (*Coming to the table with a platter of tarts.*) Wouldn't that be grand? Might make it worth planting, for a change. (*She begins to serve Walter, from the right.*)

LILY AGNES. Oh, excuse me—Mother? Properly, one serves from the left.

MARGARET. Oh, yes, I forgot. Thank you, Lily. (*She moves to Walter's left.*)

WALTER. (*Taking a tart.*) So, we'll take this measly bugger off next month. Then all we have to do is get through the goddamned winter.

ARCHIE. Aye. Get through the goddamned winter—

JAKE. (*Taking a tart.*) And try it again next year.

CURTAIN

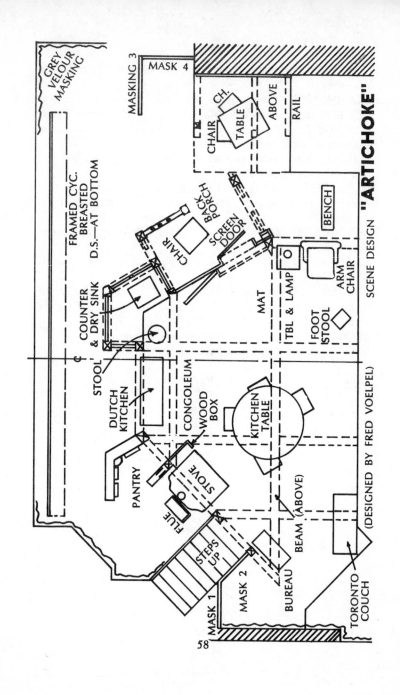

"ARTICHOKE"

SCENE DESIGN

(DESIGNED BY FRED VOELPEL)

GREY VELOUR MASKING

FRAMED CYC. BREASTED D.S.—AT BOTTOM

MASKING 3

MASK 4

CHAIR

CH.

TABLE

ABOVE

RAIL

BENCH

BACK PORCH

CHAIR

SCREEN DOOR

COUNTER & DRY SINK

STOOL

MAT

TBL & LAMP

ARM CHAIR

FOOT STOOL

DUTCH KITCHEN

CONGOLEUM

WOOD BOX

KITCHEN TABLE

PANTRY

STOVE

FLUE

BEAM (ABOVE)

STEPS UP

MASK 1

MASK 2

BUREAU

TORONTO COUCH

58

Pre-set Act I (R. *to* L.)
Toronto Couch:
    Embroidered pillow case
    Fresh shirt
    Emily Post (opened to pg. 39)
Night Stand—clothes (inside)
Stove:
    Tea kettle
    Pot holders
    Wooden spoons
    Woodbox with wood
Pantry:
    Cookie jar with cookies
    Breadbox with spongecake
    Dust cloth
    Sugar cannister
    Tea cannister
Dutch kitchen:
    Mug (for silverware Act II)
    7 dinner plates
    7 napkins
    5 butter plates
    Cups and saucers (7)
    Ring box
    Salad bowl
    Cake in covered cake plate with knife
    Bowl of frosting with spoon
    Plate with decorations
    Vase of daisies
    Wooden spoon
    Tea pot with cozy
    Lock of hair
    Scissors
    7 sets of silverware
    Extension mirror
    Stool
    Walter's towel

Dry sink:
    Shaving mug
    Razor
    Water bowl
    Dish towel
    Dish rag
    Sponge
    Dish pan with water and pot
    Bar of soap
    Dish washing liquid
    Sauce pan
    Ladle
    Water pail cover
    Rinse pan
Coat hooks—2 berry pails
Gramps' table:
    Ashtray
    Pipe rack with pipe and tobacco
    Matches
    Glasses
    Newspaper
    Sewing box
    Box of envelopes
Gramps' chair with footstool
Kitchen table with 4 chairs
Porch:
    2 milk pails
    Walter's boots
Jake and Archie's table:
    2 chairs
    2 tea cups
    tea pot

Off—Right:
Duplicate Air Canada folder
Plate with toast
Coffee cup with coffee
Duplicate cord for Gibson's box
Gibson's book (for Act II)

Off—Left:
Water pail
Slop pail

Milk pail
Fodder pail
Carton of books
Brown bag:
    Aztec calendar brooch
    British Naval Battles book
    Alligator bag
    Folding cane
Suitcase
Umbrella
Raincoat
Potato sack
3 plates
2 spoons
2 forks
Breakaway cup
Chair
Shoe rag

Strike:
    Cake
    Decorations
    Frosting bowl
    Flowers
    Apron
    Walter's towel
    Skillet (same size as broken one)
Set:
    Plate of tarts—dutch kitchen
    Biscuit pan—dutch kitchen
    Gibson's towel—dutch kitchen
    Broken skillet—in dish pan
    Gibson's clothes—nightstand, suitcase, hooks by stairs
    Pot of stew—stove
    Plate of vegetables, cutting board, knife, pealer—kitchen table
    Deck of cards—Jake and Archie's table
    Gibson's books—kitchen table
Clear Dutch kitchen counter of everything except:
    7 plates
    Mug with 7 sets of silver
    7 napkins
    Plate of tarts
    Biscuit pan
    Salad bowl